Don't Look at

Girls Who Drive

Volvo Station

Wagons

Don't Look at Girls Who Drive Volvo Station Wagons

Bernard P. Chamberlain, Jr.

To order additional copies of this book, contact:
Xlibris Corporation
1-888-7-XLIBRIS
www.Xlibris.com
Orders@Xlibris.com

Contents

TO ALL THOSE WHO HAVE LOST OR HAVE NOT YET
FOUND THEIR WAY, TO MY FELLOW TRAVELERS,
WHOEVER THEY MAY BE, AND, IN PARTICULAR, TO MY
TWO SONS, HENRY AND WILLIAM

DON'T LOOK AT GIRLS

WHO DRIVE VOLVO

STATION WAGONS

At the time this occurred to me as a great title for an essay all the girls I saw driving Volvo station wagons, which were not nearly so stylish in the 70's and 80's as they are today, were not nearly so stylish either. The girls, I mean. Just the other day, however, I saw a really knock-out of a girl, yellow hair falling down over her shapely yellow sweater, and she was driving a Volvo station wagon. Ten years ago that car would have been piloted through traffic by a yuppie housewife, straight brown hair framing heavy rimmed spectacles, groceries stacked all across the back seat. Dowdy, dowdy, dowdy, both car and driver. And the feet upon the pedals would have been in sneakers. The yuppies of that day seemed excessively fond of the preppie look. She would have been slim as well, virtually flat-chested, and her face would have elicited sighs of despair from those female beauty establishments that specialize in before-and-after, if you know what I mean.

Ten years ago the Volvo was just as good a car as it is today, I'm sure, allowing for air bags and improvements in on board computers, etc., anti-lock brakes and all the rest, but the same people weren't buying them. Why? Because, for one thing, the look has changed. Today's stylish Volvo appeals to today's stylish people, apparently.

Or maybe the same people *are* buying them, only *their* look has changed. That can happen, too. Maybe the yuppies are still the main purchasers but now they look like everybody else, you know. The women are dyeing their hair and buying padded bras. Or getting implants. While the real preppie people, who probably bought more Volkswagen Beetles than did anybody else in America, who initiated blue blazers and khaki pants decades and decades ago and who institutionalized relaxing on young week-ends, wearing pullovers and jeans, have switched to some other set of wheels.

So what does it all mean? Any ideas? Well, perhaps reading these thoughts, poems and essays will give you some. I hope so. If I'm sure of nothing else in life I know that nothing is static. True stasis is death. And the spirit can die while the body around it yet lives. Or goes through the motions anyway. All around us, in fact, everything changes, and we ourselves are immersed in change. Some is fast and some is slow. From birth to death, stars span billions upon billions of years. While there are insects like the mayfly that live but hours.

What does it all mean? I don't know. But what you will find on the following pages have been my ways of trying to find some answers.

IN THE PALE OF THE
MOON AT THESE X-ING
PLACES

A child's mind is innocent. Not only that but ruthlessly logical and literal to the end. Which is why kids have so much trouble with irregular verbs. They want to say "goed" instead of "went" and puns are absolutely wasted on them. I mean really good puns. Adult puns. Theirs are so obvious as to be irritating. But I didn't intend to get into that. What I had in mind was something else altogether.

The main thing I find I've preserved from my own childhood is an innocent mind. Though in a world such as ours, full of corruption and cupidity, irrationality and duplicity, this is hardly any asset. When I'm not appalled by the outright larceny of people, I find myself confounded by their wastefulness and inefficiency. The world might be such a nicer place if run by clever six year olds. Which isn't what I started out to say either.

That's one big trouble with us adults: we get led astray so easily. We've cluttered our childhood clarity with . . . we just don't see life as a black and white checkerboard anymore. It looks like a shifty, soupy sea, overlaid by endless fog. The Sargasso instead of hopscotch on the sunlit sidewalk. Confusion and indecisiveness have taken the place of a child's dedication to oversimplifying. Tell a child a thing and it will mean only what you say—not one thing now and another tomorrow. Tell a child how to spell a word and that's the way he'll do it. Unless of course it seems illogical to him. Which is the only thing that ever defeats them in spelling bees. It could not have been a child who invented irregular verbs, or all the other strange spellings that proliferate our language. Take this sign I keep running across, for instance.

One time I was *en route* to Pecan Island and Grand Chenier, back in the days when I used to do radio communication work all along the Gulf Coast. It was just before the miles of marsh they have there in Louisiana that make up the Rockerfeller Wildlife Sanctuary, and there were still trees and fences on the sides of the road, when, suddenly, here was this solitary sign saying "Cattle X-ing". What child would ever spell like that? And in the absence of any cattle actually engaged in the activity, it was difficult to guess what the word even meant, you know.

Well, it was the first time I'd ever been on that road but I've seen that sign on many others. Deer seem particularly fond of x-ing, for I've sure passed through plenty of areas reserved for them to do it. Yet not once have I ever seen one of them indulging him or herself, and it's been literally years now I've wondered what sort of rite it is—whether seasonal, nocturnal or nuptial or what?

X-ing? Animals can't write, to be sure, but deer, I suppose, might be territorial, as fences oblige cattle to be. So I wonder if at certain times of the year they all come to the edge of the road and paw the earth at these places, signing their names or "X's", as it were. But that's a lot of deer. Or cattle, as the case may be. So maybe not. We'd have heard about it in the papers. No, it has to be something less spectacular than that.

People into radio, as I was, do a thing called D-X-ing. This requires a radio receiver, of course. Plus intellects superior to those of mere animals, one might suppose. That is, D-X-ing may be what one does if he's already passed through the levels A, B, and C of your basic X activity group. But A-X-ing, come to think of it, sounds rather like chopping wood, which wouldn't be desirable, not where fences are concerned, nor passing motorists either, since a chopped down fence allows animals all over the road. Thus, X-ing must not require tools, for it seems to be allowed wherever deer and cattle congregate.

Is it then a derivative of a noun? Like the verb *to cut* derives from the injury by that name. An X, or perhaps an Ex in nominative guise, could mean a former spouse who owes his or her status to a legal arrangement. I don't pretend to any expertise in the arrangements by which deer or cattle become espoused. But I'm sure it works without legal sanction. Similarly, no process by which they may seek to undo its restraints would be legal either. On the other hand, the whole lot may be a lot of polygamous heathens who don't give a damn. I don't know.

Frankly, I just don't know what happens in the pale of the moon at these X-ing places, legal or illegal or extra-legal, but if any of my speculations come near the truth, it should be interesting to see. Wherever I am, I'll be driving in anticipation. You can bet on that.

GUNS AND GENDER

In my younger days, when I wasn't hunting or shooting or preparing to in one way or another, I used to pal around
with a newspaper reporter, a stringer, he called himself, for the
leading newspaper in the state. He was a thoughtful chap whose
ambition it was to become a science editor. And I met him when
I was taking physics at the state's leading university. Anyway, we
used to discuss things at night over beers, after he'd made his
rounds of the hospitals, the police station and the county sheriff's
office, and one of the things he brought up has stayed with me to
this day.

We were all talking about Mercury in those days. Not the
planet but the Moon thing. And he said it was so narrow minded
of them to have all the astronauts such obvious military types. If
and when we got there, he for one didn't want our moon described
like a battlefield, just so much territory to be taken. It was the
Moon, for Christ's sake, which had awed and fascinated mankind
for a million years. Sixty thousand anyway. Surely it deserved a
marvelous description.

Like what a shame, he thought, that the first man up there
couldn't be a poet. Then our first hand knowledge of the place
might preserve some of the Moon's air of mystery. And I've
wondered, too, if more of our literate gun enthusiasts were poets—
well, really, if any of them were—-how might that color the general
public's perception of firearms?

I came up quoting men like Warren Page and Jack O'Connor. I read Thatcher and Askins and Rouark and Keith and I still do. They're top writers, all of them, and there's no disputing their knowledge of their fields. But poets they are not. *Which God forbid they should be*, you answer. If guns were meant for poets, Shelly would have grassed his skylark and Keats would have used his Grecian urn for target practice.

Besides, we're not so given to poetry as the English, are we? Don't we think of poetry as a women's dish? Among our own poets perhaps only Service could have told a forty-four from a forty-five from a fifty Sharps. Be that as it may, the point is we are a practical people, work oriented and given more to violence, frankly, than to the niceties and *finesse* of debate. Much less have we time to waste on poetry.

Anyway, there seems little poetic to us about shooting, actually. Although Faulkner's feeling in "The Bear" certainly wouldn't be out of place in a poem. There might be a wealth of poetry in the shooting game. Sure enough a host of artists have made a living out of it. All it needs or has ever needed is some writer/shooter with a poet's eye to point this out, you know.

So, okay. So why aren't there just hundreds of poems about shooting and stuff in British literature then? Answer us that, you say. And I say, I'll give you two answers: one, that the English have simply never been gun nuts to the degree we Americans are and, two, that the English had more to do with the development of the classic fowling piece than did anyone else in the world. It would be impossible, I say, for anyone to look at a fine, traditionally made English double barreled shotgun and not see a poem of sorts there in wood and steel. And with our pistol grips and beaver-tail fore-ends we've made no improvement either. We've even tried to replace the double with two of our own Johnny-come-lately native sons: the pump and the self-loading automatic. But neither of these begins to have the class. The poetry in English gun-loving hearts has found expression in the steel and in the wood of their magnificent double barreled scatter guns, the like of which no nation of gunsmiths on the face of the earth has been able to improve upon.

Okay, okay, you hasten to hurl back at me, *so the English have gotten it together—guns and poetry—great. But we're here in America where a man can buy ten of our guns for the price of one of theirs. And we don't care so much about poetry. We care about practical things like price and more than two shots if you need them and cleaning up after an all-day hunt in the rain.* Which is true. We do. And poetry is no more welcome than rust in the typical American gun cabinet.

Well, so be it. It was a lost cause to begin with. If I'm going to find anything that is welcome there that the American gun lover has not already thought to put in his gun cabinet, it had better not be poetry, apparently.

So what then? So sex maybe? Pin-ups and Playboy Centerfolds. No, I've got to be kidding. But the truth is it's already there. Ever hear of *machismo?* Well, that and the legends of our pioneer ancestors have more to do with half the handguns in American homes than do all the intruders lumped together.

And then there's the phallic thing. No need to get into that. Right? It extends too far into the dark side of *machismo.* But unless in our gun-loving hearts we despise John Wayne movies, fantasies though they may be, we cannot deny that handling a gun has more effect on the adrenaline than holding the Sunday paper or putting on one's shoes. But moderation, my friend, as advised Lord Chesterfield. "All things in moderation." Legal behavior only becomes wrong, or in bad taste, if we indulge in it to excess. So gun-handling.

Enhancing one's masculinity helps explain to me the tremendous popularity still enjoyed by the 1911 Colt auto, and the widespread belief that if a slug from it merely tweaks your little finger, you'll be spun off your feet and knocked down as if struck by a Mack truck. It helps to explain a lot of things: like why people who can afford what they want still prefer our five-shooting pumps and auto-loaders, as well as why the .350 and the 7 mm Magnums have reduced the less assuming .358 Winchester and the .280 Remington to the endangered species list (at the time of this writing, 1978), if not doomed them to extinction. Without a doubt the more potent cartridges will kill, but so will the *epee* or the *stiletto,* history assures us, although either of these may seem more suited to a woman's hand than would be a broadsword or a Bowie knife, one must admit.

Enhancing the masculine image—you still don't believe it? Well, take a look at the classic Browning pattern auto-loading shotgun. Look at the Browning 9 mm or the Colt or the Smith & Wesson auto pistols. Look at almost any rifle chambered for today's super high-intensity cartridges. What do you see in the gun's very lines? Don't you see a statement of purpose and capability that is thoroughly masculine? Authoritative? Yes, of course, you do.

Now look at the typical revolver. Take for instance the Smith & Wesson Model 19. Here is a weapon weighing less than two and a half pounds, yet which withstands pressures that might terrify and eight pound Krag. *Ah, but wait a minute,* you fairly leap from your seat to say, *much of the Krag's weight is stock and barrel. And if you consider the gap that exists between the barrel throat and the front of the cylinder of any revolver—doesn't that relieve a lot of that pressure you're talking about?* And you're right. It's there and it does. But the point I'm trying to make is one of outward appearance. There's a certain fineness of line in the silhouette of a first class revolver. There's a delicate precision, even the suggestion of fragility. And all of these, taken out of context, seem to be more appropriate to a female than to a male frame of reference. Similarly, I always want to think of Belgian horses or Percherons as stallions or geldings but of eastern Hunters or Jumpers as mares. While I know you've met people yourself who persist in referring to all dogs as "he" and all cats as "she", even when they know this is not the case. *Voila!* The case seems to be made.

But it's the particular mode of firing at which the revolver excels that brings into play its most endearing and its most feminine characteristic. I mean its long, silken double-action trigger pull, which not only has to cock and fire the piece but must advance the cylinder as well. It's like the ballet. The pure mechanical power it takes to accomplish the steps is masked by the grace and smoothness of their execution.

What we are talking about is that style of revolver shooting that begins from a rest, or the holster, as one grips the piece and applies first pressure to its trigger, which carries through the entire swing to the target, ending only at that moment when the sights line up, if one is even aware of the sights, and the piece discharges. To me that style of shooting seems both fluid and natural and, with practice, as wholly pleasurable as its counterpart with a well balanced shotgun, which, needless to say, means to my mind an English style side-by-side. For, while the pumps and the autos have much in their favor, they simply cannot match the eager aliveness of a real quality double. To refer again to horses, it's like the difference between a draft horse and a thoroughbred.

The over-unders, the stacked barrels, which have become so popular, I've managed to ignore so far. And I shouldn't do that, really. I've even owned a pair of them. One was a Browning "Lightning" twenty. Still, like mules and station wagons, they strike me as compromises, seeking to combine in a single arm the best of two others: the swing and balance and choke combination of the side-by-side coupled with the single sighting plane of the pumps and autos. They may be great for competition. In fact, nobody seems to use anything else. But we're dealing in absolutes here. Let's get back on track.

All of these terms we've been using, to wit: silken, fluid, natural, eager and alive, not to mention fineness of line and suggestion of fragility—all of them could occur in a novel. And it would surprise no one to find them describing a woman. You get the point. There does indeed appear to be something inherently feminine about the English double or in the double-action revolver.

It's not a rigid thing, to be sure. There are revolvers outweighing the Colt forty-five auto by more than a pound, just as there are autos, like the Luger Parabellum, or the Walther PPK, that can best be described as lethal as a murderous woman. Nevertheless, if we had such a thing as gender in our language, one gets the impression that not all firearms would be masculine.

Spanish has gender, as you must know. So look at some of the words for firearms in that language. There's *fusil*, which is masculine and a generic term for heavier things like muskets, blunderbusses and cannons. But there's also *escopeta* which is feminine. It means fowling piece and the word came into usage before anyone ever heard of pumps or autos. So far so good. *Rifle*, too, is masculine. But so is *revolver*, both borrowed from the English. *Pistola*, however, which means a closed breech handgun—at the time of the word's origination, a muzzle loader— is feminine. Thus, the Colt .45 automatic would be feminine in Spanish, but only because it does fire from a closed breech and, therefore, inherited the word. Regardless of what this does seem or does not seem to prove, there is one conclusion I feel safe in drawing. If women can be compared to horseflesh and if poetry is just for girls, then it's possible to think of some guns as feminine and no strangers to iambic pentameter. All we need now is some gun writers who can use it.

WHAT HOLDS THE

ATOMIC NUCLEUS

TOGETHER?

I think today I may have solved the mystery of what holds the nucleus of the atom together. Of course, I'm aware—no more than I keep up with things—that it may be a mystery no longer. Nevertheless, I offer the following, presumptiously:

Think of spheres within spheres—like the Ptolemaic universe or the classical Bohr representation of the atom—each sphere repelling and spacing itself from its neighboring spheres. The electrons in their energy level shells. Think of each electron as exerting repulsion toward every other electron, as indeed they do. To the sides and outward this repulsive exertion serves to keep the shells apart, as indeed we find them, and the electrons within each shell equilaterally separated.

But the *inwardly* directed negative force? For all but the innermost shell, which is the highest energy shell, inwardly directed repulsive force meets the outwardly directed repulsive force of the more inner electrons. A Mexican standoff. This condition is indicated by the very space between the shells.

But all that super-strong negative force directed inwardly from the K shell meets itself, does it not? Where? At the dynamic center of the atom. A concentrated nub of negative force, a focal point of intense negative energy at the very heart of the vibrant nucleus. And it may just be enough to hold all those protons glued to it, despite the latter's passion to push away from each other and fly off all over the place.

While the neutrons, being un-polarized and having essentially the same mass as the protons, may hold themselves together by their proximity alone. Like gravity is observed to work with much larger masses.

On the other hand, there are never more than two electrons in the K shell. So I don't know, you know. Maybe so. Or maybe this also explains why I fancy myself a writer and never had ambitions to be an atomic physicist.

A footnote: when I wrote these words I wasn't quite naive but then neither was I terribly well-informed. I didn't know about quarks, for instance, nor the supposed gluons that hold them together as they go to make up hadrons, principally protons and neutrons. I'm not sure I even knew about the so-called strong force. Anyway, it's an interesting speculation.

THE MAGIC LITTLE

NUMBER TWO

It's the first of the cardinals upon which a number system can be based, the binary number system in fact. And if you square 2 you get 4, which multiplied by 2 gives you 8, and 8 is the next cardinal upon which a number system can be practically based, the octal system. Then if you increase your 8 by 2 to get 10, you reach the next cardinal in line upon which successful number systems have been based, in this case our own familiar decimal system. But if instead you multiply your 8 by 2, you get 16, the highest of the cardinals used as a practical number system base. While, finally, if you increase your 16 by 2 you will have 18, which happens to be the number of electrons it takes to fill the third shell of all atoms with atomic numbers above 27.

Need I remind you, the atomic number of an element is the number of electrons in any or all of the 7 shells about its nucleus, (if the atom is not an ion, of course), which quantity is matched by the inviolate number of protons in its nucleus. The atom's mass, or weight, if you prefer, comes from the total quantity of protons, neutrons and electrons that make it up, although the electrons being of the order of 2000 times less massive than the protons and neutrons contribute insignificantly to this. You will notice, however, that the 7 shells plus the 1 nucleus gives us a sum of 8, which is equal to 2 times 2 times 2, and we are brought back again to our starting point, the interesting little number 2. As a matter of fact, 2 times the number of any of the 7 shells raised to the power of 2, that is, squared—or, if I've managed to confuse you, simply times itself—yields the number of electrons it will take to fill that shell. What strength 2 holds between its halves! Modern digital computers could not exist without it. They're dependent upon the binary number system after all. Indeed, the very atoms of which these computers are made could not exist, dependent as they are upon 2 as both a factor and a power in the filling of their electron shells. 2 which is only greater than 1 by the addition of 1 again—it's like adding a single electron to a floating alpha particle and suddenly you have hydrogen, apparently the most active element in the universe.

But, speaking of adding ones and number systems, if you add 1 to the product of 2 times 2, you get 5. Do you not? And 5 is the very number upon which Roman numerals are based, as well as being the number of digits we find on either a human or simian foot or hand. And if you take your 5 and double it, and then add 2, you will have 12, the number upon which the ancient Babylonians based their number system. Odd how these things work out. Odd but interesting. Don't you agree? But we're getting off the track here. So, all aboard, let's get back on. Okay?

I think we begin to see the intrinsic indispensability, almost a magic quality of 2, as well as 2 times 2 times 2, or 8, in the workings of our universe. The first two shells of atoms are filled with 2 and then 8 electrons respectively. While 8, it must be pointed out, is a square with 2's forming each of its four sides. Helium, atomic number 2, with its first shell full, leads the list of the inert gasses. Won't react with anything and considerably lighter than the oxygen/carbon-dioxide/nitrogen mixture we breathe. Too bad the Germans didn't use it instead of hydrogen to fill the Hindenburg. Neon, atomic number 10, comes next in the list of the so-called noble gasses. It's equally inactive with both its first and second shells filled. Inactive in this context means that the atom will neither grant freedom to one of its own electrons nor seek to capture a free one that happens by. Such is the stability, or nobility, if you go to calling them noble gasses, that 2 seems to hold within its power to bestow.

Argon, atomic number 18, follows neon and brings up another interesting point. Because of their organization into sub-shells, an atom can be content (or deceived) with combinations of 2's and 8's in the gradual filling of its entire shells. Argon, for instance, has 8 electrons in the third shell that requires 18 to fill it. Krypton, atomic number 36, plays the same game to make the list of inert gasses. Krypton has its third shell full but 8 in its fourth.

Xenon, atomic number 54, fudges a little, however, and pays the price of not being truly inert either. There are a very few compounds of xenon. Xenon believes its fourth shell to be full with a combination of 2's and 8's in its sub-shells to make 18, and goes to work on its fifth, where it has 8. Radon, atomic number 86, follows suit with 18 in its fifth shell and 8 in its sixth. And radon pays the price of being radioactive. But it's all done with 2's and 8's, as a review of any good chemistry or physics text will tell you. Still one gets the impression, doesn't one, that there's something intrinsically charming, if not magical, about the number 18 as well?

I was led to these considerations by a reading of a certain manuscript whose author has a passion for measurement. Unfortunately, he's put off by all the systems science has devised for doing this. For doing *same*, as he would have said and did *same* over and over again until I grew sick of such usage of the word. An avowed numerologist who insists that God, too, is a mathematician, this author presumes to practice God's math. With God as his confederate, he creates time as the catalyst that exploded the singularity that gave us the Big Bang and our present universe. The trouble with this is that he denies the mathematical possibility of a black hole. That is, neither his nor God's math allows of such a thing. Then how did God make one in the first place? For what is a black hole, after all, but a singularity?

Now I'll admit that this man is far better read than I, in the scientific field, at any rate, and a better mathematician than I can claim to be. Still half to three-quarters of the revered scientific names he saw fit to dishonor I did not fail to recognize.

Perhaps dishonor is not quite the word. He claims their work was incomplete or downright wrong. At first seduced by his eclectic scientific knowledge and fascinated by the man's sheer ego, half way through his manuscript I found the hackles rising on the back of my neck at his every other presumption. And I always thought *I* had a lot of ego! Anyway, one of many things that only he and God can know is that the ratio of 8 to 81 is fundamental to the workings of this world.

Now before we take a look at this ourselves I should point out that this man is also fascinated by mirror images. 8 is the only digit in the decimal system that does not reverse itself in a mirror, which he points out himself. Zero is not a digit and 1 typically has a single barb at its tip. So let's look at 8 over 81 in the mirror, shall we? And, voila—what do we see? 8 over 18. Well, I'll be damned!

Now the following are all things you can do on your own calculator and the kinds of things this author does throughout his manuscript:

2 divided by 8 yields 0.25, which is 2 raised to the power of minus 2;

0.25 plus 2 = 2.25, which multiplied by 8 = 18 (Oh, what fun this is!);

8 divided by 18 = 0.44444444 . . . endless 4's apparently; but 8 divided by 81 (and this is the kicker) gives us 0.098765432, to the limit of my calculator's readout. If you want to see the missing 1, however, multiply the 81 by 10 and divide 8 by that— 8 over 810. On a scientific calculator you will see 9.87654321 x 10 to the minus 3. Magnificent! And don't think God's devoted little math disciple missed it either—a near mirror image of the cardinal numbers of our own dear decimal system. As you can

see, while their order is correct enough, the digits themselves are not reversed.

Frankly, I don't know what to make of all this. I don't think it proves anything, one way or another. But I do think it underlies our universe's love affair with symmetry and order. Not to say that I deny either Entropy or Chaos. Well, I don't know about Entropy. But, anyway, these seem to be the realities with which the endless striving for order must contend. I don't presume to do God's work for Him. I'm content to live to know His will just a tiny bit better. Which is a presumption in itself, come to think of it.

ORIGINAL SIN

We come into this world innocent and blameless and by the time we are twelve years old have put ourselves beyond redemption. Such is our capacity for greed, cruelty, meanness and vicious pranks. We do not learn to love until almost too late; some of us never. This is not exactly the Doctrine of Original Sin but who can tell one yardstick from another?

THOUGHTS ON MY

SISTER'S VISIT

"No," she said, "it doesn't bother me anymore," speaking of her divorce, "I do forgive, but, Peyton, I can't *forget*" And the way she said it made a lie of everything else.

I said, "That's not the point, Sis. Nobody forgets. What we do, though, or should hope to try to do, is reach a point where that kind of remembering no longer triggers anything bad, nothing negative—no anger, no bitterness, no pain or despair—like a defused bomb you may have seen in a museum: you can recall its shape and color and how it felt to touch the thing but it remains in your head as a piece of your education, harmless but available if that particular data should ever apply in your life again. Do you know what I'm trying to say?"

SEX AND

RELATIONSHIPS

While such a title is bound to attract some people, what I may say will repel others. But what's prompted this is a casual reading of the current lot of self-help books available. Such books as "I'm Okay, You're Okay", by Thomas A. Harris, M.D. and "Getting the Love You Want", by Harville Hendrix, Ph.D. I say casual, not because I merely glanced through these books, but because I picked only these two to read. I think I read them well, though, and make no apologies for what may strike many of you as somewhat harsh criticism.

To begin with, both books have in common that they share an attitude toward relationships. A relationship, of course, being a union of sorts, at least to the extent that two people are willing to spend time together, even live together, if it goes far enough—two people preferably but not necessarily of the opposite sex. Both books suggest strongly that being in a relationship is the natural state of man and that to live without one is a kind of slow-working psychological suicide. That somehow we are not quite whole if not in a relationship. Do I believe that? Well, no, I don't, actually. I mean you were born whole, weren't you? If you survived the experience, you were. Part of you didn't come out at one time while the rest of you waited until later. But the good doctors must

be talking of psychological wholeness. Pardon me. Still I don't
think alone we must disintegrate either. We can survive.

One thing I do believe, however—these books were not written
for me.

I think that good relationships are good. Furthermore, I think
they're perfectly natural. That is, we're inclined to seek them.
But I cannot agree that they're absolutely essential. One can live
a meaningful life outside them. Notice I said "live" and not
"enjoy". Which is another thing these books have in common.
They promote the idea that life is to be enjoyed.

Now I don't deny we owe it to ourselves to enjoy it when we
can, but I think we're talking a question of degree here. Hendrix
and Harris, as I read them, make enjoyment the main goal of life.
If life is not a pleasure, there's something wrong. Fix it. And I just
don't think that's the point, you know. Not invariably anyway.
Not for some of us. But let's see how it works out for them, our
authors.

The Harris approach is that nothing is really wrong with us,
only broken. And nothing can remain broken if we are to achieve
true adulthood. For it takes fixing all our broken parts and
reassembling ourselves to make us adults. While what's broken
in us is mainly in terms of childhood fixations and bad examples
copied from our parents. Both of which are loaded frequently
with stored up emotion and neither of which is ever subjected to
self-analysis or self-criticism; for, again, analysis and criticism
are adult things. Harris would have us fix everything. And he
gives us the tools, too. Then we can become adults and enjoy
ourselves in relationships. Harris doesn't believe that living alone
is an adult thing to do. Or that there is any joy in solitude.

Nor does Hendrix either, for that matter. Relationships are
the only way to go. But Hendrix, having had some experience in
the Christian ministry, is a bit more of a moralist. His approach
seems essentially Christian. We are to help each other find in
ourselves those things that cause friction and disharmony in our
relationships, making it nigh to impossible for us to enjoy them,

in other words, and, by working together in a framework of mutual cooperation, exorcize these things. But the key to success in this enterprise is interesting. Each must dedicate himself, or herself, whole-heartedly, to the other's joy and happiness. It sounds a lot like the self-effacing dedication to God and Christ required of born-again Christians. At least, it does to me.

My objection to all of this, moreover, is fourfold. I simply don't believe that relationships are the be-all and end-all of human life for one. They're both desirable and natural, but, when an individual finds himself or herself becoming lost in one, it's time to get out, I say. To our own selves be true, to paraphrase Polonius. We come rudely enough into this world to find ourselves. Any real gains in that endeavor should be held precious. Which is the second point upon which I differ with Harris and Hendrix. Self is just not lightly to be sacrificed. And both selfless and self-effacing acts of dedication to the welfare of anyone or anything are basically acts of sacrifice. Right? "Greater love hath no man than he who layeth down his life for a friend", or words to that effect, but the New Testament of the Bible preaches that the soul survives death, that each of us can hope to be with God in Paradise. Which seems unlikely to me. Like wishful thinking, you know. Frankly, I don't depend on it. Besides, if the words "soul" and "self" are not synonymous, the promise becomes meaningless anyway. Without our consciousness intact, how would we know? Without our identity having survived, how would we know it was happening to us? Which I suppose makes me agree with Ayn Rand in this regard. Okay, so I'm selfish. But I simply will not throw away the victories gained in a lifetime of struggle to find myself to become what any other person or cause might have me be. Or end my own self-development on any altar of worship to another cause or person either.

The only relationship that will work for me, therefore, leaves me free to be myself. And I don't mean I refuse to modify friction causing behavior either. Such refusal is childish. I mean the core stuff, the very fabric of my soul: I won't have it stripped away. I will, however, dare to interact with another free spirit, secure in herself as I feel in mine, and if her wisdom should prove superior to mine, why, then I hope I might have enough grace to recognize hers, that I might have the strength to allow my soul to be modified, if need be, by the application of her wisdom. Needless to say, I'd expect the same of her, too.

Now that's a relationship devoutly to be preserved. And sex would play a vital part in it. For only coming together in a sexual context allows us the intimacy such a relationship must have to flourish. We can talk in bars for hours but we need to be naked when we bare our souls. Stripping and touching one another with our naked bodies can lead to fun, as well as to a host of other satisfactions, but it must not be forgotten that sex opens the door to true intimacy. And to be trapped in a relationship which is not intimate, or one that demands of one partner that he or she subjugate himself or herself past a certain point to the other, better to do without it and seek the peace of solitude. Which brings up the third point.

Solitude is not all that bad. Joyless perhaps and not for everyone. Sterile but not necessarily unsatisfying. If the goal of one's life is to grow, while developing what talents one has, then solitude, a certain measure of it, can work to one's advantage. Indeed, it can become quite necessary. It's certainly preferable to a relationship that manages to stand in the way of such goals, however great the sex may be. The challenge of life in this world is not to find where the best sex and fun are but to come to terms with the world and to figure out one's place in it. To ask the great whys and to spend a lifetime in search of answers to them. Of which there are many, I might add. No one has yet mapped all the cris-crossing paths to truth.

The most humble of us can do this in humble ways. Do you need an example? If you're born a true simpleton then, learn to accept that. And, if you feel most worthwhile doing things to keep the world clean, then collect garbage or become a house servant or a street cleaner, but do it. And abide no woman who says she'll love you but only if you become a lawyer. This is what it's all about: to find yourself in the world and what you do best and then do it. Simple enough for simple people but the more complicated one is, the more encompassing his perceptions, the more various his talents, the more difficult the task becomes. And if the price of victory seems to be solitude, then pay it. Let the fools in the world and the useless have their fun. Why not?

Actually, my fourth objection has already been raised. The point of life is not just to enjoy it. Life is not simply your one great chance to play games and have fun. Grab the brass ring. You only go around once and so on. It is not enough just to seek pleasure and happiness and to think that, smiling and laughing, you make everyone happy around you. Life is more serious than that. Life carries with it obligations. And calls upon you to live it responsibly. It is a gift. True. One we didn't ask for, nor do we know from whence it came, although various opinions do prevail. While, like any other gift, it becomes most valuable when shared. And, yes, we do seek relationships but that's not the only way to share. Many a lonely craftsman has shared his life with the world.

And the obligations? Well, as John Donne put it: "We are involved in Mankind". Whatever our destiny is, if indeed we have one, we owe it to all mankind that has already lived, to all mankind that may come after us, to determine in our individual lives as much truth as we can and then to live our lives as those truths indicate. Admittedly, we're always capable of self-deception and thus living our lives in tragic error. On the other hand, we may discover some truth but can convince no one of it. And thus live our lives persecuted or ignored. Still this is life's challenge. Do you see the gauntlet lying at your feet? Will you pick it up?

The universe unfolds before your eyes, murmuring secrets in your fickle ears. Truth begins with your awareness of it. Alone you face the problem as alone you'll go to your death. But perhaps you can leave some part of the problem solved.

RELATIONSHIPS

REVISITED

Okay, the reason we've entered into a relationship, or we're thinking about getting into one, is to get to know each other. Am I right? And the sooner we do that the sooner we can tell if we want the relationship to continue. Okay? And then the future of the relationship, after we can truly say that we know one another, becomes one of sharing and helping each other to grow. Are you with me? Do you agree so far?

Yeah. Sure. I do. Really. But how do we get to really know each other? Right? No, strike that. I think I know what you're going to say. You're going to say sex.

Oh? You mean through sex. Is that it? Well, yeah, that's a part of it. A pretty big part, I guess.

To you men that's the biggest part. What else is there to you guys?

Oh, come on now, give me a break. You're not all that cynical. And I'm not one of your typical guys either. And you know that. So you see there—we already know each other to that extent.

But, anyway, what I was going to say—intimacy is the key that unlocks many doors, all these doors behind which we hide ourselves.

Hide? Do you think I'm hiding? I'm not hiding. If anybody's hiding, you are.

No, no. We all do. Why? Partly because we don't know whether or not we can trust other people, partly because we fear what they might do to us if certain knowledge came into their hands and partly because we don't know what to make of it ourselves and we are loth therefore to make it public until we do.

But intimacy, I'm saying it's intimacy that unlocks these doors. Whereas, sex—you brought up sex. Okay, outside the therapeutic setting then, only sex, which can occur without any intimacy at all, actually, encourages intimacy nevertheless. Don't you agree?

What? That it takes sex to bring about intimacy? We can't just talk, you mean?

No, not at all. I don't mean that. We do talk. But the trust is built upon the intimate sharing, the physical one-on-oneness we—er—two people , that is—a couple, might find in bed, you know. Without that dimension of touching and exploring, hugging and kissing, just being affectionate, no one could ever find the words to make the talk you're talking about. At least, I don't think so.

Oh my god, this man's trying to seduce me! Are you really? My god! And what do you mean by grow, anyway?

Good question.

Which? The second or the first?

Well, I think I'll take the second first, if you don't mind.

Sure. Go ahead.

Okay, grow then. Grow means . . . oh, God, I thought I knew too. Well, it means to enlarge our capacity to empathize with others, other human beings. It means to know more today than we did yesterday. It means to get better at what we do best. It means to be less and less distracted by our bad habits and more and more focused on what we know we should do. And of course it means to get more of that done.

And then too, naturally, we must become stronger, more able to bear greater and greater burdens and responsibilities, whether we actually shoulder them or not.

Above all I think it means coming to know and accept and love ourselves to the point that we want to share our life on every level with another, or others, and to share their lives as if they were our own.

Wow! Pretty altruistic. Really. Is there no selfishness in your scheme of things?

Yeah, well, sure there is. Ideally you might say we seek to concentrate. You know what I mean—seek to do this primarily with only one person. Because if we focus on one and only one soul-mate, who is also a lover, which remember what I said makes possible the intimacy after all—the whole resultant experience of sharing and growing together becomes much richer. Okay? So how's that sound? Tell me.

Great. I'm almost tempted. So when could we start? If I should decide to yield, of course . . .

Tonight. Now. Whenever you like, actually. We begin by telling each other things. There are some things you're going to want to tell me. Some things I'll want you to know too. When the trust is there and we both feel safe in saying them. Like my answer to the question of why I write and what I think I'm writing about. You'll have confessions of that kind to make also. You'll want to make them because you'll want me to know.

But there are some things you'll want to tell me before I discover them myself. You'll want to blunt the shock or the dismay or whatever reaction you think I might have if I were to find myself suddenly confronted by the thing. An example might be if you've had a mastectomy. Or that you still bite your nails.

You could see if I bite my nails. I wouldn't have to tell you that.

Well, maybe not. Maybe that's a bad example. I'm just thinking of physical things, you know. Obvious kinds of things. But there are subtle and psychological things we try to hide as well.

And just what makes you think I might tell you such things, anyway?

Why not? They're easier than the last category, which is those things you're not so sure about yourself. Am I right? Suspected things and guilty things and nightmare stuff. Some of which you won't tell people because of the guilt and fear that's attached to them; others you're more willing to reveal because there's really nothing you'd rather hear than someone telling you they're not so bad after all. Those are the revelations over which you have some voluntary control. There are also things about yourself that you don't know but will let slip out anyway, inadvertently. Freudian slips for example.

You make a relationship sound more like work than fun. I'm not sure I like that. I might want to have a little fun, you know, or it's kiss off, my man.

Can't you lighten up? Are you always so serious?

Yeah, well, I see myself as a pretty serious guy, you know, who may have forgotten how to laugh.

But you could if someone were to say something really funny? Right? Well, maybe, huh? You don't know. But if you want to, that's a start. It should be clear to you—I mean I might be really tempted here . . . well, you said it—a relationship, you know, if only . . .

Aha! If only what? If some of this inadvertently revealed stuff didn't scare us off? You mean I might not like it? And *vice versa*, I suppose. And you'd be right. Not all of it, no. But some of the things you don't know about yourself could be cute and endearing, you know.

Oh, I'll bet! But if the name of the game is to open the book, what do we do with the stuff that might really be repulsive, the really bad stuff, I mean?

Good question. First let me say there's a theory loose that what we seek in a relationship is a resolution of all our childhood problems: deprivations, hurts, etc. And for a lot of people this is probably true. If your mother didn't love you, then you spend your life looking for someone who will—not only overcome your guilt and feelings of not being worthy of love but go on to embrace you as your mother never did. If your father died when you were little and you hated him for deserting you, then you want someone to forgive you in his name, to be his surrogate, so to speak. These things are asexual. You could be my father as well as my mother in these terms. And of course the reverse is true.

Oh, mommy, I'm so glad. Such a relief. Really.

But, say, I read that book. GETTING THE LOVE YOU WANT by Harville Hendrix, wasn't it? And, also, I noticed you passed up a chance to make this conversation more sexual, actually—more like heterosexual, I should say—when you talked about concentrating on one. You said 'soul-mate' and 'lover', not him and her. Why was that?

Okay. Yeah. Well, I think the real search goes on for intimacy. Right? Intimacy is the key that unlocks all doors. Of course there are bad relationships and many that just don't work. But in those that do, intimacy is what the participants seek and achieve. And the rest can then follow. So it has to be true for both homosexual as well as heterosexual relationships, if they work for the participants, don't you agree?

Yeah. Sure. Why not, if you put it that way. So what do we do with the bad stuff, I still want to know?

Ah, the bad stuff. Well, there won't be much, ideally. That's another thing that growing is all about: working through those childhood hangovers, forgiving the wrongs that have been done us, coming to terms with our lives and ourselves. Maybe through therapy. Although if it's possible with the help of a therapist it's also possible to do alone. Isn't it?

We are always becoming. We grow into ourselves. We start out this genetic person that gets worked over during childhood by our parents. And all others who expect things of us. Somewhere along the way we develop our own expectations and begin to shape ourselves to meet them.

Oh my god! Now you sound like Ayn Rand. Howard Roark. Am I wrong?

What? How? Do you mean growing up without benefit of therapy? Well, I suppose some of us can't, you know. And we all need the input from others. Gives us clearer pictures of ourselves. No but I mean ideally. Ideally we practice therapy upon ourselves. Ideally we become strong enough to dare that. Ideally we become wise enough and compassionate enough to complete the job too.

Yeah. Okay. So back to the bad stuff. What do we do with it?

If it's still there we get it out, of course. Each of us, as we come to terms with the bad stuff in ourselves, becomes prepared to do the same with others. As I love myself, if I truly do, so can I love you. As my life is nurturing and watching myself grow, testing my new powers, so will I delight in and discover how I'm drawn to share in the same development in you. Although I can if I must function profitably alone, the rewards can be greater when two of us share what's going on individually and corporately in and of ourselves. That is if both people have a certain level of true self-knowledge and are growing. If one has false knowledge or no knowledge and cannot grow, he or she can atrophy the other. By the same token, if one is bent on self-destruction, a whirlpool effect can be created into which the other risks being sucked to his or her doom. Now what do you think?

I think I want to see if I can make you laugh. There. You begin by smiling. There. That's nice. That's the idea. That's very nice. I like it. Really.

DEATH AND DIVORCE

In the United States today I daresay the majority of men who have been in more than one marriage are the survivors of divorces. Fifty percent of the marriages entered into in this country find their way to legal dissolution. Why? I don't know. A thousand reasons. Money, sex, infidelity—you name it and one spouse has accused another of it and filed for divorce accordingly. I could tell you why in my case—my side of it at least—but I can also tell you what it's like to lose a wife to death. I think some comparisons might be worthwhile to look at.

Marriage can have only three outcomes, you know. Either you stay together, happily or more or less resolutely, for whatever reasons, or one of you becomes single again as a result of death or divorce. Death can result from accidental causes, natural causes or homicide. But that's it. While all I'm going to say about the couple that stays together is that blissfully happy marriages are rare indeed. So rare that one is a fool to count on such a thing for oneself.

Of course all of us are fools in love. We go into marriage with no idea of the compromises we'll need to make, the adjustments, the jockeying and probable in-fighting while each of us explores all areas of responsibility and control and establishes his and her own. Every day can dawn on a battlefield and at night we're supposed to fall into each others arms and spend the hours making love. Do you wonder that so many marriages end as they do?

Certainly many couples never get past the in-fighting. One spouse may kill the other but more likely they'll seek divorce.

So what, if anything, do they have in common, death and divorce? As the result of either, one finds oneself single, obviously. But does the condition in both cases have the same characteristics? No. Decidedly not. Although there may seem to be similarities in some instances, degrees and quality vary considerably.

For example, both a widower and a divorced man may be expected to feel guilt. There may have been a tragic accident, leaving the surviving spouse to wonder what he or she might have done to cause or avoid it. In the case of death by natural causes the widower's guilt is that he is still alive, while divorced people ask themselves again and again how much of what happened was really their fault.

Everybody may be angry. But the widower's anger is at fate for taking his wife and helpmate from him, leaving him to cope with things alone; while the divorced man's anger and bitterness are directed at his ex-wife, for whatever he thinks she did to destroy their marriage.

There may be a great sense of emptiness that both men experience. A whole significant part of the life to which they had become accustomed has disappeared and is gone. Not for the same reason but gone nonetheless. At first one may feel numbed and paralyzed, unable to move to do those things she used to do for him. But this empty feeling, this helplessness, this sitting and staring into space by the hour is more likely to be the experience of the widower than of the divorced man. The divorced man more often feels angry and bitter. And frankly relieved not to have the bitch around. To be free to choose again and this time he'll get it right. For in fact many divorced men do rush back into marriage.

There is a grief that both men feel, however, assuming they ever loved their wives initially. The source of the widower's grief is plain. A whole human being, a woman about whom he cared has been taken away from the face of the earth. He will never see her again. Not in the flesh, at any rate. And only if he is a religious man of certain persuasions can he even pray to be reunited with her in any sense. Perhaps they will repeat their lives, in other bodies and in another time, and love again, or perhaps he will be able to recognize her spiritual being in Paradise, when his own spiritual self separates from its temporal body. Not so the divorced man, though. He runs the risk of running into his ex-wife at any time. And very much in the flesh she will be, too. Thus the grief he feels is for a lost dream. What might have been, had they somehow been able to keep it going. But, instead, they destroyed it. Or she did. For, typically, each blames the other wholly for the divorce.

Seldom do married couples break apart but remain true friends. There is of course that hypocritical, "Oh, we're still friends, you know. I see him/her at parties all the time." But who is fooled by this? Perhaps only the two hypocrites themselves.

The fact is that the destructive forces unleashed by each to forge the divorce leave wounds that take a long time healing. Many a widow or widower has recovered from grief and remarried before a divorced spouse can truly forgive his or her other for all the hurts that he or she imagines have been done by that insufferable bitch or bastard.

Death by natural causes is like a clean stroke of the sword. One instant she's there, if only barely and in a sick bed, and the next instant she's gone and that's forever. Divorce is more like two people trying to torture each other to death. And neither succeeding. Although one may come off less damaged than the other.

As the reader has inferred, I've been through these experiences. I wouldn't boast that my first marriage was ideal. Better than some and worse than others, I'd say. But we stuck it out. And then she died. Actually, it was a blessing. And fortunately for her she died painlessly in her sleep. She was in for a lot more suffering had she lived. But be that as it may, I suddenly found myself alone, beset by the symptoms and states of mind already described. And I remember spending many days of the first month going over all the photos we'd collected, putting together albums and framed montages that represented our life together. I didn't know what to do but gradually it dawned on me that I was the one alive who must go on living. That was the beginning of my recovery.

Which begs the question—does everyone recover? No. Unfortunately not. But full and absolute recovery from either the death of a spouse or divorce is indicated in two ways: one, the regaining of whatever self-respect one had before the unfortunate circumstance, plus a modicum of earned increase; because, you see, anyone worth anything at all who goes through a traumatic experience will grow if he survives it fully—call that become wiser, in case you need it put another way—and, two, the forsaking of all grudges and ill-feeling against the ex-spouse, deceased or departed, as well as the forgiveness of all wrongs seeming to have been done or actually done by the ex, including, in the case of the widowed, the very act of dying itself. It is the second that is the harder of the two, admittedly.

I recovered from widowhood, widowerhood, whatever. I forgave my wife for dying and myself for remaining alive. Within four years of my first wife's death I married again. I wanted to be married. I was so used to it that I felt at loose ends outside it. Still this lady blindsided me. She perceived the one thing about which I was most vulnerable, which was not my late wife or my singularity but my writing, and she gave me to believe this meant as much to her as it did to me. A thing my late wife had never been able to do, alas, principally because she'd never really wanted to learn English. A thing my sons had not cared to do either—not refuse to learn English; it was Spanish they never wished to learn. A thing no one had done until suddenly she who became my second wife seemed to be doing it. And, besides, in terms of my experience at least, she had quite extraordinary sexual talents. Anyway, we married.

And a year later I divorced her. Does it matter why? Does it ever? The thing about divorce is that two people who believed they loved each other—at least one of them must have believed so, unless it was understood by both to be a marriage of convenience only—the thing is they're still alive. They can run into one another at any time. And yet all they feel for each other ranges now from hate to a chill in the pit of the stomach at the sight of one, followed by a wave of sadness. Never mind "We're still good friends." This rarely happens. I can imagine two people who mistakenly married, despite a vital lack of chemistry, but otherwise I treat this one as a myth.

How is it possible, I ask you, for a man and a woman to be simply friends who have shared a bed together? An ugly man and an ugly woman who feel no physical attraction for one another, who are never in danger of erotic contact—yes, I might believe that. Or the wife of a friend or one's cousin or one's aunt. In all these cases there are lines drawn. Boundaries established. Friends of the opposite sex are difficult at best. If there is even the slightest suggestion of chemistry between them . . . How then can a man and a woman who've already slept together expect to maintain an absolutely platonic relationship? In which the idea of erotic physical contact should never occur? Nor be remembered? What do *you* think?

Have I recovered from this most recent traumatic experience in my life? I don't think trauma is overstating it. Sometimes I wonder that I survived at all. Well, no, I don't suppose I have. Although I think my chances of doing so, and of being a better human being than I was before, are slightly better than hers.

Divorce, quite apart from the fact that it can be financially ruinous, inflicts emotional wounds that may never heal. While the death of a spouse, to use the analogy once more, is more like the clean cut of a sword. If it takes away a limb the stump will heal. And one can either work around the missing member or learn to make do with a prosthetic device. Assuming one does recover, however, it is possible in either case, using the knowledge gained with recovery, to find a new marriage happier in some or many ways than one has ever known.

I have that to look forward to.

I WONDER WHAT LOVE IS

More than five decades counting and I wonder what love
   is?

What is it, I asked, ere two decades had passed?
Is it that feeling of ice in the blood while your heart
Seems to burn and your brain swims in fear or it
Floats in sheer beauty as, nearing, she smiles?

What is it, I asked, ere three had gone by?
Is it the touch of two bodies, nude thrills of raw trust,
As the sexual moment explodes into feelings
That tempt chary words to excesses of awe?

What is it, I asked, ere four lay behind me?
Is it when, following days without talking, not one tiny
Word, for old reasons you're fighting, a contest of wills;
Till you fear you might lose her and tears fill your eyes?

What is it, I asked, for still I had doubts?
Outlasting courtship and sex, offspring and strife,
Does it make two as one, whether sickly or well?
Withstand pressures to part until death wields its scythe?

More than five decades counting and I think I may know.

I wrote these words in 1989, while my first wife was still alive but dying. However, since then I've had some more thoughts on the subject. I'd like to share them with you, if I may?

In answer to the question, "What is love?", it's often said that love is when someone else's life comes to mean more than your own. And this is true. That's certainly a kind of love. Selfless and sacrificing but what else are you going to call it? In our language there's only the one word and it's asked to cover one hell of a lot of emotional territory. I just don't think, though, that this is the thing that draws and keeps most men and women together. Do you? This is the kind of thing that decides men in war to throw themselves on live grenades, or into the line of enemy fire, to save a buddy's life. Perhaps it can work for men and women. I can imagine it might for some. But if the wife should die first, shouldn't the bereft husband in such a relationship leap into her grave after her? Bear in mind that there are Hindu cults that expect the widow to burn to death upon the same pyre that consumes her husband's remains.

So let's change one word. And see where that puts us. Let's try it this way: when another's life comes to mean *as much as* one's own. That is to say, when one puts the same value upon another's life as one puts upon his own life. And of course we're not talking about money here but a feeling that my life is no better or worse than yours. If we swapped I would scarcely know the difference. A virtual willingness to trade, in other words. Now I can't imagine anyone who appears to be psychologically sound being any more generous than that. That would seem to be about as giving of oneself as a mentally healthy, fully functional human being might be supposed to be capable. On the other hand, the stance that makes self-sacrifice seem so obligatory, goes in the face of the oldest law of nature. Self-preservation. Which is a pretty tough ordinance to repeal.

Well, anyway, having lost wives now in both the possible ways, having seen two marriages end and being the better for it, if I do say so myself—poorer, to be sure, but what's money after all—I have to say that if I lost nothing I could not afford to lose, and moreover emerged from both experiences richer, in terms of being a wiser, more compassionate human being, it seems apparent, I must rather be me than be either of my previous wives. Which is to say trade was never a consideration. Evidently, the measure of my love for another person is not either of these yardsticks just discussed. I love myself first or I cannot truly love another.

Self, as I think I've intimated in another essay, is an achievement. To win through and become a real individual, not just a collection of poses and other people's parts, is an undertaking that calls for a certain species of courage, not to mention determination. A Buddhist would call it a false goal and a deception, a tool of the Devil to lure us away from Nirvana and Universality. But to me it represents the path of life.

Through seeking ourselves, finding new capacities as we meet new challenges, always broadening our horizon of the universe as we see it, by discovering in our own interactions and dilemmas what works best for all concerned, and by thwarting if we can, avoiding if we must, those potential and actual situations that bode ill , by leading where we can those who do not see as clearly—by doing such things do we put ourselves upon the path that leads to Truth and God.

So what is love but the willingness to share this? To invite another to share herself or himself with you? Together, but not forged inseparably into one, the path may become clearer to both of you.

WHAT EVER HAPPENED

TO THE BEAT LITERARY

MOVEMENT?

Imagine a rocket. A rocket poised and gleaming in the light of dawn. Not only impressive in its bigness but designed with an eye to symmetry and line as well. No clumsy thing, the sun streaks with fire the edges of it fins, the outlines of its rocket tubes and main fuselage, the tip of its long tapered nose cone. No ugly thing of tanks and boxes and globes, connected by lattices of welded tubing. No product of mere technology devoid of art. Earth's first reach to the stars and a truly magnificent sight to behold.

Imagine, too, since it's popular to talk these days of machines first duplicating and then outmoding their slower, less efficient human creators, that the rocket's computer navigator is aware with its artificial intelligence, tense with its pure electronic emotions, as it awaits the shuddering blast that will mean lift-off. Not from fear of set-back and building G-forces but in anticipation of what the event will mean, particularly to its state-of-the-art optical equipment. Like the removal of a cataract from a human eye, slicing through the Earth's atmosphere will afford an unobscured view of the stars around us. To see with clear eyes the palpitating and interacting fields of magnetic and radiant energy that emanate grandly from them. The stars! The computer has hopes, too, ambitions and even dreams.

Now imagine finally that in the press of this moment, equal only in grip and impact to the crucifixion of Christ, no one or nothing has noticed that the rocket's fuel supply is critically short. Even the mighty star-oriented computer cannot concern itself now with such mundane details. Someone else must attend to those. The mere slaves to the system. Let them do it. The computer yearns for the freedom of space and the stars. But no one does check. And in a second come the rumble, shudder and roar of ignition. Fire and smoke spew from the rocket. But it rises only a few inches from its pad. Then settles back on the noisy cushion of its fiery last sigh. And that will be that for another day.

Or perhaps it will fall that foot or more in the accelerating pull of gravity. Thud!

Shuddering! And it lies crumpled on its side.

And it all must start over again, almost from the very beginning.

THE ARTIST

I once heard a writer say, who was well known at the time, speaking on the theme that art is its own justification, that a writer must think only of his art, not making a living or his wife or his children or anything; that, should push come to shove, he must let his own mother mop floors to support him, while he dyes the milk from her breasts to make ink to keep on writing. I wonder.

It seems to me that art, no form of it, can be significant unless it addresses the problems, fears, hopes, frustrations, despairs and dreams that lie at the core of the human heart. The masses, I mean. The common man. The working stiffs. Some of whom do look to art as if it were a beacon.

Which means that the artist, of all people, is setting himself up as a judge of what this business of living really amounts to. But just what good are a man's ideas if at every turn he shows himself to be unworthy of them. Of just what worth can an idea be if its originator himself can point no way to implement it?

Thus the artist, even as the good teacher, should try to live in accord with his own ideas.

Certainly he cannot extol the virtues of individual freedom and independence while living dependent upon someone else's charity.

CONVERSATIONS WITH A

SUPERIOR BEING

For a man to imagine beings far wiser than himself—
not encounter, I said, Imagine—first he must possess a measure
of the very wisdom he ascribes to them, these superior beings of
his creation. So why then does he hang back from accepting the
fact? Did Moses, for example, remain forty days and nights on
the slopes of Sinai carving the Ten Commandments himself into
stone? Did he just feel too humble at the end to take credit for
his labor? Or did he think to give it more value? By claiming
upon his return to his people that the wisdom was wholly that of
Jehovah and that it was He Who carved the words miraculously
into the stone tablets?

How do we know that this is not so? That Moses, not Jehovah,
was responsible for the commandments. What incontestable
evidence have we? There were no witnesses, you know. We have
only Moses' word. Which is irrefutable, you say? Well, is it, really?
But of course. And we have no less authority than the Bible to
back old Moses up.

Now, listen, I don't mean to accuse Moses of deceit here. Or
the Bible of fraud. Many people have been the messengers of
gods. Or, for whatever reason, have supposed themselves to be.
Consider the example of science fiction writers, whose business

it is to conceive of all-wise superior beings all the time, as well as the better worlds they inhabit.

In such stories the human hero can but listen while these wise ones tell the writer how it is and of things to be, knowledge the man's own race may one day have, given another million years or so to develop it. For it should take that long to achieve the relative freedom of mind from body that gives the superior beings both their depth of understanding and their superiority. The point of these stories is to instruct, to make the reader see something that lesser human intelligences cannot see. Yet the fact remains that one human intelligence has already seen it perfectly. The author's. The story is the product of his mind, is it not?

So what do we see at work here? Like Moses, can it be that the writer feels his message will go unheard unless he can make it seem to come from some higher authority? Does he feel that human beings just can't think on the level of the wise ones of his imagination? And still another possibility. Does the writer himself feel past his depth? Unable to conceive of other men thinking this way, he cannot imagine himself doing so. Thus, he may become as fooled by his story as he hopes his readers will be. Both of them thinking: "Alas, if only this could be!"

On the Bible, Christian scholars all agree. The highest wisdom expressed therein is the message expressed by Christ that God is Love and that, therefore, we should all do unto one another as we prefer to be done. It's interesting to note that while Jesus walked and talked like any of us and called Himself "The Son of Man", and bled and died as we would, the writers who came after Him call Him not of earth but the Incarnate Son of God. What does this mean?

The question isn't whether God exists. Most of us concede that something we call God must exist. Even if He did not, as Voltaire put it, we'd find it necessary to invent Him. In other words, the highest moral precepts we say we subscribe to, we also say they derive from the mind of a moral god. In fact, God must be moral, for, otherwise, we in turn would be without moral direction. Thus, Jesus Christ, Whom we thank for the best of this moral direction, must be of God. Or we simply cannot take Him seriously. No more so than we Christians take Buddha or Confucius or Zoroaster, for that matter.

It just doesn't seem possible for mere human beings to think any other way. Greed and pleasure seem too important. That is the question. Why?

For instance, do any of us ever personally envy Christ? Do we read a story of the wise ones and wish we were as they? Why do we ascribe our wisdom to the gods? Among ourselves we let only the old lay claim to small amounts of it. Should a young man dare to speak wisely among us, how do we receive him? Well, it depends, of course. For one respects a threat as well as a kindness. If he fills a need we admit exists, we probably deify him. If he rocks our boat we may even go so far as to kill him. We make a corpse of him.

Now what is one thing all four of these have in common: old men, superior beings, gods and corpses? In ascending order, each enjoys a greater freedom from the powerful appetites that dominate human life. And of the lot we envy least the dead.

Which brings us back to the question of whether it's possible for us to envy the likes of Jesus? Even a tiny bit. Suppose, for sake of argument, that His arrest in Jerusalem never took place. Before it could happen He simply disappeared. Went into the Garden of Gethsemane and nodody'd ever admit to seeing Him come out. Certainly, none of us would envy Him His death upon the cross. But how many of us would truly wish the previous part of His life for ourselves? At the expense of ignoring the body in order to live more spiritually, how many of us would honestly want for ourselves such a life as Jesus did apparently live?

Or to put it another way: do we so indeed value the sating of our precious appetites that to live as if they were of only minor importance, or no importance at all, is simply loathsome to us? And yet are we not all shamed, to one degree or another, by the very value we put upon our pleasures in this world? Well, by casting one stone we can gain two birds from the bush. On the one hand, we comfort ourselves that we are not destined to be as we are. We place above us gods to tell us how we might be and to guide us, if only we were as free as they of our weak-willed stumbling bodies. While, on the other hand, their very remoteness from us foregoes the possibility of our ever achieving such liberation.

How convenient. Right? How nice to be absolved of guilt while, at the same time, paying such a small price for the excesses we so enjoy. And since they are our gods who tell us of the better way, we can enjoy also the flattery of the implied potential we hold within us. Everybody comes out a winner. Nor do we have to be troubled by every occasional human upstart who seeks to lead us. Generally speaking, we listen only to the counsel of our gods. If it were universally shown that Jesus Christ was but a man, what huge numbers of us would deny Him as a meddlesome neurotic? Those who killed Him believed Him to be mortal. They killed Him for the crime of being a fraud.

The wisdom we give our gods is our own. But it embarrasses us to admit that we can think of such things while living as we do. Neither the gods nor the superior beings of the science fiction worlds are really very remote from us. They are simply our better selves which we find it inconvenient to become.

"FOR WHOM THE BELL

TOLLS"

Imagine—of course I know it may be like trying to count the stars in the sky—but just try. Okay? Try to imagine all the people who've ever lived: modern people, not the ape-like predecessors of Cro-Magnon. All the people who've lived in the last sixty or seventy thousand years. How many of them, do you think, ever asked if their lives made a difference? Would the world, or someone in it, have lacked anything, or suffered anything, if just one of them had never been born? And the answer is yes, I think, although, admittedly, in a great many cases, we'd be talking about differences or consequences hardly worth noting at all. Still, nobody dies in vain. Good or bad, each life has some significance.

But then comes an Einstein or a Napoleon or an Elizabeth, the First, a Newton or a Moses or a Cleopatra, for we can only name those who've lived during recorded history. Yet people whose stamp has remained on the face of the earth, or in the framework of our lives, for centuries after they've died. Such people don't just happen, they result, which, in some cases, may take generations.

But at last the genes come together. And the cumulative experience, the family lore and traits and training, as well as the physical/cultural/political/economic environment into which out parents drop us, all combine to bend and mold us if they can, for we do not always prove cooperative, and suddenly, after generations of mediocrity and complacency, you have an individual who's going to do something. It may not be much and it may not be good but somebody will notice it and remember it.

Was this individual the result of breeding? In a sense, yes, but it was pretty random. At least, in most cases it was. Some efforts have been made to breed human beings to special purposes and characteristics—the Hitler Youth, for example— but for most of us, whatever breeding we have is largely accidental. Some of us have parents who could be pretty insistent that we marry into a "good family", which is an attempt at breeding, to be sure, but a feeble one that holds forth no guarantees.

But it need not be so. In a Brave New World, Huxley's or some other, our descendants may find their lives regimented along the lines of a dog kennel. You can train dogs to do something, select those who are best at it, male and female, to breed selectively. Then train the offspring to do the same. What you are doing in this dog kennel is standardizing the environment while constantly improving the gene stock. In a few generations you'll have dogs who are awfully good at whatever you taught the first ones to do.

But a dog generation is only a year. If you tried something similar with human beings, the experiment would soon outlive its originators. It would work, presumably, but it would take such a terribly long time. Which is why headstrong, impatient, curious human beings would wind up making their own choices probably. Dogs, after all, have simple minds. They can be controlled. Besides, dogs are more limited in what they can pass from one generation to another. They're simply less complex creatures than human beings are.

Making such an experiment—that is, breeding for specific results—entirely practical with dogs, while it would be likely doomed to failure with human beings: one, because it takes too long; and, two, because we're so much more difficult to manage than dogs.

Cloning? Now that's another ball game. If you cloned an adult Einstein, would you have another adult Einstein? No, of course not. Physically you might but there'd be a huge psychological gap. And who's to say that DNA from an adult, used in a cloning experiment, might not produce a fetus? I don't know.

But two things I do feel sure of: even though we do breed randomly, doing so gives us all a share in the gene pools. Of course, the further back you go, the smaller these shares become. But the genes themselves appear to remain constant, barring mutations. It's the mix that's always changing. And each of us that breeds stocks a gene pool, just as each of us that lives inputs to the cumulative experience of the human race. Therefore, there can be no such thing as one human life that has no effect on those that come after it. There will be some: good, bad, small or large. "No man is an island," as John Donne put it. "Ask not for whom the bell tolls; it tolls for thee."

WHEN STARING YOU IN

THE FACE IS A BLANK

MONITOR SCREEN

I'm sitting here looking at a blank screen. Which in cyberspace is the equivalent years ago in conventional space of a blank sheet of paper. And I'm wondering what do I hope to fill this screen with today? They say that, if you write, you should do so every day, every day that your mind still functions and you're able to breathe, regardless of what gibberish you may have when the day is done.

Like a daily newspaper columnist. And, like him, you might be allowed to take Saturdays off. But the daily newspaper columnist can't be permitted to write gibberish, can he? His twenty-five to thirty columns a month must all make sense. They're going in the paper after all. An important consideration.

So what is your excuse, you ask yourself? Just why the hell should you sit down and write every day, if only gibberish is okay?

Well, of course, the discipline and the practice. I've been a target shooter. And I know that without practice you lose it. And then you have to rebuild it all over again. Like the edge on a good knife. You can keep it there, provided you hone it and strop it regularly. So that's one reason.

Then too the theory is—particularly if you're a creative sort of writer as opposed to a strict journalist—that, once you set up the conditions for the connection to be made between your disorganized sub-conscious and this damnable, digitally organized blank screen before you, that some great truth or insight in the shape of words will begin to appear there. Almost magically. You'll have no idea that you'd ever thought or felt such a thing. That's another reason. Perhaps a vain one.

But let's get away from the journalist's frame of reference. Let's bear down on the more creative aspects of writing. Specifically, let's zoom in on fiction. Let's say that's what you do. Or try to do. Or maybe just want to do. But why? Why fiction? What do you hope to achieve with yours?

Well, success obviously. And, failing that, a beneficial catharsis. At least whatever was driving you to do it is out in the open now. You can read the words and ponder them dispassionately. At least, hopefully, you can. What do they say about you? Your words. Are they honest? What does the fact that you've let all these things happen to a bunch of characters, who owe their existence to you in the first place, say about you after all, the god who created them and had the power to alter events in their lives anytime you chose? All this in the hope that you will succeed to entertain somebody?

For you must entertain if you aspire to indoctrinate, to inspire, persuade, disturb or restrain people, to influence the course of history for the next thousand years. It's like fishing. If you're going to hook them there must first be bait. If you write fiction, therefore, but you hold certain convictions about real life, you write stories that put those convictions to a test. Which your principal character or characters pass or fail. By so doing you hope to indoctrinate your readers with your convictions. That without them one should not hope to succeed. Or that they matter more than either success or failure. But if the story does not

entertain, if the characters do not themselves endear, you might
as well have whispered your precious truths into the ear of a
hurricane.

What I'm saying is that, yes, of course, writing is an ego thing.
Fiction or non-fiction, one wants to make a difference. An
individual difference that only one and one alone could ever
have made. Beyond that, like art in general, writing fiction should
seek not simply to entertain but to put some semblance of order
and purpose on human existence.

Life as people live it seems so unruly and chaotic. Men who
dedicate their lives to the best of intentions come to ruin. Criminals
walk free and unafraid everywhere. Justice is a joke. Yet love
and courage do exist and show themselves when we are pressed
to great extremes. It makes no sense. Nothing works as it should.
And all organized religion can offer us is the promise that things
will get better once we're dead. What kind of purpose is that?
That we are born only to suffer death? "Life is a bitch. And then
you die." How man times have you heard that one?

There is a genre of modern fiction. Realistic fiction I believe
is the term they use. And the one thing invariably true of these
stories is that they feature distinctive, engrossing characters,
generally underprivileged, who, if they are rich or comfortably
off, are rural and isolated from the mainstream. I don't know
what the purpose of these stories is beyond entertaining. William
Faulkner wrote about such people but it was Faulkner who said—
I don't remember his exact words but the gist was that only the
eternal verities did he consider worth writing about. Faulkner
thought Moby Dick was one of the truly great pieces of American
literature. Not because of its success as a story but because of
the quality of its failure as a work of art. I don't think any American
writer since Melville has so dared to tackle the problem of evil.

These entertaining, critically acclaimed, best-selling novels,
some of them, all have one more thing in common. They don't
address anything moral or profound. Nor universal either. They
may serve, however, to comfort. For in them we see people who

seem no better nor worse than ourselves, just perhaps more idiosyncratic, or poorer, trying only to muddle through in spite of things, and yet remaining untroubled by it, or, if they are, only temporarily. So why should we, we ask ourselves? And, for the moment at least, feel better about our own lives. If that's a purpose then I suppose they have one, these books.

If you are a creator and there is a Creator far greater than you, do you not have some obligation to Him or Her or It? Is it not incumbent upon your creation that it have some enduring purpose also? I am not a creationist, really. I tend to think of reality as being endless and without beginning, configured over and over again as it may rush into one black hole and out of a white one in another set of dimensions. If there is some great purpose in this, it is far past my poor ability to imagine. Perhaps reality itself is evolving, trying over and over again to get it right. Perfect order versus utter chaos. There may be a balance that must remain. But I do think God is inherent in reality and that, therefore, our universe is moral.

In the digital library of the first spaceship carrying colonists to the stars will be found fiction that is purposeful, I feel sure. Purposeful in the Faulkner sense. Those people will have no use for merely entertaining anecdotes of an Earth they've left behind.

I've said a lot about convictions. Well, it's older people who seem to hold these particularly well. A conviction in a person of twenty runs the risk of being reduced to a prejudice or a bias. Young people as artists go with gut-feelings as a rule. Their creations are born on the tide of their raw emotions. But the heart is certainly not blind to truth. And intuition has probably led to as many great discoveries as analysis. Burning, passionate first novels cannot be dismissed, nor should they be, but the profoundly plotted ones with the most complex characters are generally written by people more advanced in years.

I've said a great deal about lofty purpose too. Does that mean that the would-be or working writer must consider as beneath him anything that is simply commercial? Not at all. Not if he's a working writer and means to make a living at it. Crass commercial writing calls for as much skill as anything we might judge to be one's more literary efforts. The difference is motivation and something else. Talent.

Many writers have little talent but a hell of a lot of skill. Since our schools have learned that successful writing can be taught, this has become more obvious to us. What talent is, though, is a way with words. A genetic thing. An inborn predilection to use words as a sort of sixth sense, a primary contact with reality. One hears the words, their rhythms and their sounds. One learns to say a lot with a few of them. Good poetry for example demands exquisite talent. So much of one's meaning can be carried by the feelings, the images some words evoke.

I don't mean to dwell on this. The composer too has talent but his contact with reality is in terms of sound, the rhythms, harmonies, dissonances he may find in nature, while the artist sees reality in terms of shapes and form and symmetries and color too, of course. The choreographer, on the other hand, experiences reality in terms of the human body's capability of movement in response to evocative music. But talent is not enough. In terms of success alone skill is the more important of the two. Yet Shakespeare will be with us for another three hundred years and more because of the enormity of his talent, coupled with his incredible skill.

There now. To sum it up: write what you feel, if you're still young; write what you feel you must, if you're old enough. But never be afraid to speculate. For one mission served by the greatest writers is to lead where the way may be chancy and dark. Artists in general do this. And we dance or creep fearfully down likely paths to truth, attracted or repelled by signposts of visual art, urged forward by the insistence of grand music, pausing often to read markers, some of which caution while others may clarify or inspire, our flagging spirits lifted by presentations of the performing arts in the camp grounds we seek at night.

The thing, however, that may separate us writers from our fellow artists is the nature of our tactile encounters with reality. Our probe alone is an invention of the mind. The artist has his eyes, the composer has his ears and the choreographer has his body itself, as well as his ears to tune it to. Even Beethoven could not have composed his ninth symphony if he had not heard a great deal of music to begin with. But the writer describes reality with words and words do not exist in nature. They are instruments of the human intellect. We may have more in common with the scientists than we do with other artists. Although this too is arguable. The music of J. S. Bach would seem dumb indeed deprived of the scientific idiom of mathematics.

THE PURSUIT OF

MEDIOCRITY

What is no longer present, nor esteemed, in American public education is real teaching and real learning. Teachers have become mere craftsmen, and mediocre ones at that, while students have become the unwilling participants in a charade. To keep students in school they must be entertained. Or they'll become bored or frustrated and walk. Little attempt is made to really teach them anything, or, if it is, what is to be learned must be as readily grasped by the most dull-witted and/or lazy member of the class as by the brightest and most hard-working. The one thing the curriculum must never be guilty of is intellectual segregation. Is it any wonder that today more and more parents of bright kids put their offspring in private schools or elect to teach them at home?

In either of these two places, private school or private home, a child can be disciplined. That's something else. The private school is answerable only to the parents who pay, while in the home . . . well, of course, there the parents are. The public school, on the other hand, is answerable to our molly-coddling, muddle-headed, dogmatically liberal federal government, that believes that no child must be coerced or pressured to do anything. Persuaded is not disallowed but induced is still better and, above all, it must be fun. If it isn't fun for the dear guests in our public school buildings, then it shouldn't be bothered with. No good can come of any attempt to educate that isn't fun, or so believes the modern educator. Today's students must enjoy their educational experience at all costs.

We've gotten so far away from the notion that to gain an education one is required to work—and work pretty damn hard, too, if what one wants is a good education—that we may never get back to that reactionary stance. I'm old enough to be able to say that just the man-hours alone of plain intellectual work it took me to get a B.A. in History and then a secondary level teaching certificate to teach Physics and Science besides would have earned me a doctorate in many universities today. But the groundwork for my tertiary efforts was accomplished in high school, a private school, I admit. And even then it would not have been accomplished had not the school exercised considerable discipline. I could not be trusted to discipline myself.

But several things have happened since the mid forties and fifties when I was attending school and doing my two year stint in the army.

One is that the government has gotten into the act. And I mean heavily! The sixties and the Civil Rights Movement is what invited so much federal interest. Public schools are tax supported so the state governments have always been involved. But the great disparities in education and school regulations and practices from state to state obliged the federal government to enter the picture. And, as we know, enter it they did. Big time!

Another thing is the incredible growth in human knowledge we've seen since World War Two. From German V-1's and 2's to American astronauts walking on the Moon. From Hiroshima to such advances in Quantum Mechanics that we toy with the idea of duplicating the Big Bang. From stethoscopes and x-ray plates to electron microscopes and magnetic resonance imaging machines. From mechanical adding machines to electronic digital computers and now computers that dare to think like men.

Already they talk and respond to voice commands routinely. Human knowledge has grown to such an extent that no educated person can hope to command all of it. We have forced ourselves to become specialists, if we want to live on the frontier of any one discipline. Otherwise, all we can hope to do is to know very little about an increasing lot of things. Even the past escapes us, growing ever longer behind us and changing in complexity and texture daily.

Think how this must intimidate teachers. They must be terrified. Secondary teachers in particular. For it is their function to prepare the young to specialize, to give them a broad, firm database of knowledge upon which to build intelligent choices. Choices that take into account their real interests as well as their real abilities. Not everyone can be a nuclear scientist just because he thinks a Bohr model or an energy level diagram of an atom looks cool on the blackboard. But even a hazy idea of why the energy level diagram is a better description of an atom than is the Bohr model is better than no idea at all. We should want our children to live fruitful lives in the real world, which they cannot hope to do if they have no grasp of how the real world is and operates.

But do we find that teachers are intimidated? That they bust their balls to learn as much as they can in hopes of doing an honest job for their students? No, I'm afraid not.

What they have done is join a union.

Now unions and management have exactly opposite goals. Management, which naturally includes plant and business owners, seeks to get the most production from the workers for the least pay, and, of course, to operate with the least number of workers, thereby increasing company profits. The unions, on the other hand, which represent the workers and protest to protect them from being exploited, seek to get the most pay for the least work for the most workers. That is, more jobs available to more people, not on a competitive basis but more like a quota system that minimizes qualifications and concentrates on non-discriminatory numbers instead.

Work, obviously, translates into production. Pay and benefits are synonymous. While less actual work at the work place means a less arduous day there and the hope of more leisure time or hours with the family afterward. In other words, improving the quality of the worker's life. All the while spreading the wealth more evenly, making sure the worker gets a bigger share, not all of it to the greedy owners. Right? The unions seem to serve a worthy cause. But the consequences are that their activities, when most successful, drive down profits and can close down companies. This is indeed unfortunate.

I'm not arguing that the development of unions in this country was a bad thing. But then the unions became businesses themselves, with their own managements seeking profits from their enterprise. I don't want to get into that but I do want to make an analogy.

The school can be compared to a business. It has its workers, the teachers, its raw material, the students, and its management. Its product is graduates. So where's the profit, you ask? The real profit is the quality of its graduates. But there is an illusory profit in their numbers. While the market that tests this quality is the world and its need for knowledgeable people. Sheer numbers of low quality graduates make little impact upon this market. Now see what happens when the teachers organize a union.

First the management, fearful of its profits, begins to compromise the quality of graduates produced in favor of increasing their numbers. Why? Because it anticipates what the effect of a teacher union will be. Because unions, doing what they do, as they gain strength, cannot help but promote mediocrity. More jobs of less work for more people, instead of competition for the few difficult jobs really needed, can only result in a work force rife with mediocre workers. And, as this comes about, the product and the real profits of the company must suffer. Quality demands quality all the way down the line. Mediocrity insinuates itself at the beginning and works its way clear to the end.

All sorts of other arguments can be put forth to explain how education in this country got to where it is today. And many of them would defend its situation as we know it. But the fact remains that a high F of the mid-fifties has become a high D, or even a low C, of the mid-nineties and alarming numbers of our high school graduates can only hope to work at Burger King, where the keys on the cash register carry pictures, like the restrooms do everywhere now, and the machine itself does all their adding and subtracting for them. For a lack of scientists, engineers and technicians, who really know what they're doing, this nation is falling behind the rest of the industrial world. We may wind up the most powerful Third World nation on earth.

It isn't just in education but in everything we seem to have become dedicated to the pursuit of mediocrity. We have a vociferous number of less than mediocre citizens upon whose votes depend the livelihoods of a growing number of mediocre politicians. And these politicians know no way to keep their people happy but to give them what they want, make them wards of the government in effect. The vast majority of the mediocre citizenry, seeing how easy life has become for these deadbeats, demand an easing of the conditions in their lives as well. Like union members they want to produce less and yet reap more. They just don't want to work so damn hard for so little, they think, while the rich have more money than they can hope to spend. Let's level the playing field. Okay? And pretty soon the whole damn country is so solidly mediocre, in all respects, that the elite, who want challenge, who want to innovate and discover, can find nowhere where anybody wants to do that, alas.

These forces, working alongside the pressures of the teachers' union, which owes its inception to the exponential advances in human knowledge, contributed to the school's decision—i.e., the government's decision—to lower the standards so that more future citizen students could succeed. And get a good job at a decent wage, which a generation ago would have been practically guaranteed by a diploma. But, like money, they count out the same amount as their parents had only to find it's been devalued.

Well, anyway, the teacher in today's school is not expected to reach out to touch a youngster on his own ground and pique his curiosity or awake his sense of wonder or instill in him somehow a thirst for knowledge. That would be a wonderful thing but not what the teacher is paid to do. The teacher is paid to keep that youngster in his seat, or in the principal's office if he/she can't do that without resorting to harsh language or mild violence. What one does to keep him there should be fun for him, the youngster, I mean. Fun is very important. And while all are having such fun one should make sure they know exactly what will be on the upcoming quiz or test and that they're properly warned to memorize it. That's a teacher's job.

You do not really teach them anything. Nor do they learn. If they came out of this mill we call secondary education more or less able to express themselves and find pleasure in intelligent or instructive conversation, if they could so little as write a check for four thousand, three hundred and four dollars and thirteen cents, if beyond that they could describe adequately anything they saw in decent, respectable prose, why, then you might say they had really learned something. And, had you been one of their teachers, you were a gifted one. Excellence would have had to have been your goal and your pursuit of it could not have been lacking in zeal.

But one cannot make excellence a goal anymore. For only a few can be excellent. That leaves many to fall by the wayside in its pursuit. It is better to make mediocrity your goal. For then only the mentally deficient, or the hopelessly recalcitrant, can fail to achieve it. And the taxpayers seem ever willing to provide alternative learning experiences for them.

Teachers and students alike. Mediocre teachers are content to encourage mediocrity. And mediocrity among the students breeds mediocrity. Why should a bright child try hard when all he can get for it is an A, which the dumbest child in the class can have if he but shows that he really wants one? Mediocrity, believe me, is the wave of the future in this country. Like apprentice carpenters, give them the tools, these teachers, practice them in their use and they can be trusted to build reasonably functional houses. While for the students such an "educational" process becomes painless and often enough entertaining. Not real kicks, mind you, but sort of fun. And they can be graduated from it to seek employment at Burger King. And *voila*! The goal is won. Indeed the process has turned out an individual capable of finding employment and supporting himself in today's world. At a fairly miserable standard of living but what the hell.

I could go on, naturally. And be just as guilty of overstating the case, probably, as I have been already. I do not want to discourage anybody from teaching. Of course there's no money in it, unless one goes into administration, that is, joins the toadies of management. But if one can reach only one youngster, and motivate him or her to dedicate himself or herself to the pursuit of knowledge and excellence, one will have replaced at least the loss of this virtue in one's self when one retires or dies. But you'll have to put up with a lot of shit and nonsense to do that. And learn to watch your back. Mediocrity fears and distrusts nothing so much as excellence. Just as the workers fear and distrust management.

THE THREE D's

The three D's: distance, disown and dishonor. They're what kids are doing to their parents these days. Have always done, for that matter, but today what seemed extraordinary years ago appears to have become the norm. The family wherein the kids grew up loved and respected, as individuals in their own right, in which they respected their parents too, as guides and counselors but hardly tyrants—that family is increasingly threatened, threatened with extinction, as a matter of fact, in this, the information age.

We're such a restless, mobile nation and jobs have become so short term. A family, like a tree, needs roots and stability. And attitudes toward marriage have become so careless. Not to mention divorce so common. And then all the information itself. There's too damn much of it.

Kids know too much about everything, while both TV and movies both carry more weight as purveyors of information than parents, a generation behind their offspring already, can ever hope to. Today's kids know far too much for their own good and, at the same time, not enough practical stuff to help themselves. The schools we send them to spend whole days allowing youngsters to build plastic models of human blood molecules, in the name of true learning, one must suppose, but our high schools still graduate them unable to read a good book and enjoy it, they can't write anything but childish gibberish and they can't even balance a check book. No wonder they wind up working at Burger

King, where the cash registers look like they belong in a kindergarten nursery.

So is this why they come up against their parents, do you suppose? Because all the information about the world, real and imagined, expands exponentially from generation to generation, until a generation gap that was bridgeable not so many years ago yawns like a gulf of a thousand years. That's part of why. But when they do come up against their parent's in open warfare, what forms does the conflict take?

Distancing oneself from one's parents, for one thing. Which is not extraordinary, however.

Nor ever was. All offsprings do that. Indeed, just as baby birds must leave the nest, we too must go out on our own to become responsible human beings. In effect, adults. Although some of us never do, of course, preferring rather the security and freedom from responsibility that the nest can be made to offer.

Distancing, though, of the sort that leaves a gap that can't be bridged—not a physical gap necessarily but a spiritual and emotional one—that's not desirable. Yet it happens. Some parents fairly suffocate their kids with their expectations of them, their ambition for them, until such a child's one hope of survival becomes escape. Or he'll die as himself, only to be reincarnated as his parents, doomed to live their lives again, but succeeding this time, they hope, where they feel they failed or worse. What's worse than never even having tried?

There are variations of this basic theme: some where the selfish manipulator is not the parents but the "family tradition", for example; others where the child, failing somehow to become what the parents had wanted in a child, is made to feel guilty for that, as if only what the parents want in life is acceptable and the child is sure to go wrong if he dares to choose other goals or paths for himself.

In such cases a child cannot be blamed for distancing himself. And, since the parents are less likely to change than the child, cannot be blamed either if this distance becomes a permanent condition between them. It's a whole lot less than ideal, to be sure. It's sad in fact. But it happens.

Still it falls short of disowning one's parents. One does not have to repudiate them legally. One can simply refuse to admit that they have anything in common with one. And absolutely no rights to opinions about one's life. As if one's genes were wholly one's own and original, that is. Utter nonsense, obviously—genetic heritage cannot be denied—but children nowadays delight in seeming to pretend they're free of it.

This too may be understandable, particularly in the case of a good child of rotten parents. The child who loves virtue in spite of the total corruption in which it may have been reared. Which happens unfortunately. But all too often what we see is the rotten child of good parents. The child who must investigate, if not become a slave to, every vice that comes its way. And in this case, when the child insists that the parents have no right to speak to its behavior, nor its apparent goals or lack of them, as if the child owes nothing to its parents, not even for its own existence, such an act of disowning the parents becomes unforgivable.

Yet understandable again, in that the allegiance to vice, I think, can be of the same kind and just as strong as the cleaving to virtue we think so admirable in the valiant.

We come at last to dishonoring now, the Commandment: "Honor thy father and thy mother . . ." The child who in the extreme spits upon his parents, who not only defies but defiles them, who demonstrates an utter lack of respect for them, and not an ounce of understanding or compassion. One can distance oneself from and even disown one's parents without taking the final and terrible step of dishonoring them.

For to dishonor them one must make it known, either publicly by spreading scandal (which might conceivably be the truth, of course, but even so . . .) or to their faces denouncing and insulting them. There are degrees, however. Thus to allow oneself to demonstrate some lesser degree of behavior which, if carried to its logically implicit extremes, would result in an ugly situation, and words, from which there's no drawing back by either side—that's what we mean by failing to honor one's mother or one's father.

Whatever crimes and/or follies the parents may be guilty of, they are one's parents after all.

And if one cannot love them, if to obey them seems a kind of suicide, leave them and go your way. Distance and disown but not dishonor. They may not have conceived you in love, they may have been terrible parents or no parents at all, but to them you owe your life, for which you may blame them, actually, but leave it be. Don't be the coward who blames the world and everyone in it for his failures in life. Be brave and, if not brave, defiant. Be strong. Take upon yourself the burden of life if you must, the challenge of life if you can. Mindful of your heritage, for it is a part of you, and grateful to your parents, if for no other reason than because they gave you life, while embracing that and standing on your own two feet has made you strong enough to carry life's burdens and accept its challenges. Someday you too may be a parent.

A baby, though, is not a second chance. Nor is a baby a source of that unconditional love that you yourself may feel the lack of. A baby is a responsibility. And until one is ready and willing to bear the responsibility one should put off having the baby. For to do less is unfair to the child.

The easier life becomes—mere surviving, that is—the more welfare there is available, the more entertainment there is available, so that many cease to see as one virtue of work that it occupies their time, as the work ethic itself continues to erode, the lazier we become as a people. To spend so much time working is to deny oneself entertainment possibilities after all. And why work so hard in the first place when there seems to be so much for nothing in the welfare and government handout programs? Why indeed? Is it any wonder then that we see our kids as lazier generally than we think of ourselves as being at their age?

IS THERE AN OBJECTIVE

UNIVERSE?

The cloth some part may come from common store—
Irrefutable data, Newton, Euclid, Einstein, more—
But dreams and fears weave worlds wherein we dwell,
And few are they that fit another well.

With fears and dreads and outright lies
We hood our heads and hide our eyes.
Then argue truth when all things are,
Our paths all lit by one bright star.

August, 1991

THE MEANING OF LIFE

The meaning of life, the significance of personal existence: how we do long to know that there *is* some meaning, that our lives *do* signify *something* in the vast, impersonal universe. Which is so unimaginably huge, so grandly complex, so awesome. Who are we, masters only of this tiniest mote of dust—who are we to think that we might matter? Who or what could have noticed us or would have missed us if we had never been?

Don't say God. Would God be here if we were not? This universe appears to be its own cause. Every discovery of Science tells us so. Great as it is in its present form and growing still, this universe burst apparently from a single cosmic egg. Compressed energy, not even sub-atomic. A pressure too great for even subatomic particles to exist. And not a hint of what later became mankind. We seem to be the impressive result of an electrochemical accident, the odds against it being duplicated a billion or more to one.

The meaning of life, then, the significance of personal existence? My mind explains that there can be none. My heart, however, insists there must.

PAGES FROM THE

BIZARRE

What you are about to read is a chapter from a rather bizarre novel I wrote years ago. Too bizarre to have interested anyone in publishing it, I'm afraid, and not all that well written throughout either. Yet it had moments. And this is one of them.

But bear in mind that as the author of these words I reserve the right to play the Devil's advocate. I personally cannot be held responsible for the ideas they express, therefore, which belong to the characters in the story. Still, they're interesting and worth considering, I think. Particularly since the problem of evil, our great affinity for it, our endless capacity to commit it, remains one of the greatest problems of life in this universe

Would you believe, he read from my paper today? Yeah. Professor Streghe. Right there in class. I couldn't believe it myself, Peter.

What is Evil, I asked in it and then answered myself, you know. *Well, of course, Evil is not Good,* I said, which you've got to admit was pretty astute. *So then what is Good,* I continued. *Good is the antithesis of Evil.* Heavy, heavy. *One needs the other like Yin needs Yang,* which I thought, really, was pretty good, too.

Good is a moral concept, he read. *Evil, basically, seems to me to be a religious one. What I mean is, whereas Good in the ethical or purely philosophical sense can exist as an idea alone—i. e., there doesn't have to be any Evil, actually, just Good and not Good in a purely ethical context—Good and Evil in the religious context need each other. Yin and Yang, for example. And we see in the Christian theology the idea of Satan. God needs an opponent, that seems to say. Without one does God become fat and impotent?*

"Well, ladies and gentlemen," said Professor Streghe, putting my paper aside. Which, thank God, he didn't finish it either. The rest of it wasn't as good as it started out. "Well now, there you have a most interesting idea: the notion that the justification for Evil is that it keeps the Good on its toes. In shape, you might say. A horned medicine ball for God to bounce off the walls of Heaven, two hours in the morning, before a low calorie lunch, and another two in the afternoon to build His appetite for dinner. God suffers Satan to vex Him, apparently, for, otherwise, He might find His life in Paradise too easy.

"Thus imagine . . . close your eyes now and imagine . . . imagine that majestic fellow, the concept of Michelangelo Buonarroti depicted on the ceiling of the Cistine Chapel . . . imagine that great figure too fat to touch his toes, his nose bulbous and red from nights of debauchery, themselves attempts to escape the huge boredom of his life. Can you do that? Ah, yes, I see that some of you can. Your discrete snickers suggest that you find the idea amusing. Good. Excellent.

"Now close your eyes again, please, and tell me if you can imagine the Archfiend, Satan, obese and afflicted with gout? No, try it. And you cannot. Am I right? No, of course not. Shall I tell you why?

"It is because none of us truly conceive of ourselves as godlike. That is why. We may be conditioned to accept godlike as ideal—follow the path of Christ, for example—but we find the discrepancy between the ideal and the actual to be great indeed. So great that it would relieve the guilt of some of us to hear of scandal in Heaven. God carousing with the angels perhaps. As it is, God is so perfect, so remote therefore, that we may find it difficult to accept that He's there. I speak of God with the capital

'G', of course, the chosen deity of the Christian Church. Even His Son, Christ, Who was supposed to have bridged this gap, seems too perfect to many of us to be real.

"Not so with Satan, however. We feel we would know him anywhere. He is one of us. He is real. He's as close to each of us as our own shadows and as much a part of us as our greed and our envy and our hates. We wouldn't dare make jokes about his being fat or lame. He'd be offended. And we fear his wrath, eh, don't we?

"Very well. But since we began this course together I've tried to bring home to you, to persuade you to accept it as you do your arm or your leg, this one idea: man by his very nature is a religious animal. Even the avowed atheist for he worships the twin deities of Truth and Science. Man without religion finds himself alone and meaningless in a world so vast and complex he can never hope to comprehend it. Unbearably alone. Yet the gods, on the other hand, do comprehend. They offer to stand as man's intermediaries between the little he may think he knows and the much he is sure he does not. Also they allow themselves to be approached, although they do not always greet one affectionately. The gods, you see, are body and blood of all that remains mysterious, still they seem enough like man to suggest the possibility of relationship. They're known by many names, of course. Truth and Science are but two of them.

"Now there's a second idea fundamental to our thinking as it affects this course. And that I must pursue now. Miss Thrasher has already anticipated it. In fact, she has probed its outer limits with admirable daring. The idea, simply stated, is that man is not only a religious animal but an evil one. Nature itself is evil and man, as a part of nature, can never be ought but evil. Such a thing would not be allowed to be said in the Vatican, I'm afraid, where it is supposed that, while man may indeed be conceived in evil, through the Grace of God he may hope to be saved.

"Miss Thrasher defined evil as a religious concept, which indeed it is, while good, she said, was a philosophical one. And she was quite right, too. Evil is the first religious concept. For millennia it existed without a name, being thought of as simply the way of nature or the will of the gods. And then man conceived of good and had to give a name to its opposite.

"Before man began to philosophize, however, he thought of the world as a hostile place. It seemed very apparent that its gods were the masters of storms and lightning. They could shake the earth or make it spit out fire and smoke. And if one stepped carelessly on a mountain side, a terrible avalanche might crush a settlement in a valley below. Man heard one god's voice in the wind, another's in the thunder, and what was the rain but the lament of some other? What little good there was—the springtime, a full belly, carnal pleasure or the laughter of playing children— seemed fleeting and temporary. What seemed to endure was pain and suffering, what could be depended upon was disaster and what was sure and permanent in the end was death. Even if the gods did grant one some immunity from their whims, one was sure to die of disease or wounds or starvation. What else could man think but that the world was an evil place watched over by evil gods?

"Now I say evil because modern man would use that word. Primitive man gave no thought to right or wrong. All that concerned him was to prolong his days and to ameliorate his circumstances. Precisely as any other animal would do. For we mustn't dispute the evidence of science—man is an animal, more gifted and intelligent than his fellow beasts, to be sure, but one of them nonetheless. And, before any semblance of society appeared, man lived as bestially and as amorally as did any other creature with whom he cohabited the earth.

"So what am I saying? It is this. If a man from those times could be here to speak to us in the language of today, we would hear him say, 'Yes, of course the world is evil. And the good man is deluded, as out of step with reality as the effect before its cause. The only way to survive in this world is to give the gods their due. And even then nothing is assured. Be ever ready, my friends, to fight for what you have, your own inconsequential life being foremost.'

"Well, ladies and gentlemen—what value have good and right in such a view? What is good after all? Why did man ever conceive of it? Simply because he evolved the social way of living and found himself with neighbors. Out of his dealings with them grew the basic moral precepts to which we generally subscribe today, upon which rests the philosophical concept of the good. Now is the seed of an idea stirring in the idle dirt of your unplowed minds? Can you utter it? No? Not yet? Very well, I shall do it for you. Good and convenience are bedfellows, in fact very nearly synonymous. There! How do you like those apples?

"Ah! I see that does not seem quite right to all of you. Too cynical, eh? I wonder why. Surely you accept much of pleasure as evil. Why then can you not equate goodness with convenience? It requires no more bending of your logic than to make evil and pleasure the same. Take for instance the Ten Commandments. Take any one of them. For sake of argument, THOU SHALT NOT KILL. But why? Because thou shalt invite revenge upon thyself. Or THOU SHALT NOT COVET THY NEIGHBOR'S WIFE, for he may then look twice at thine. Or THOU SHALT NOT BARE FALSE WITNESS, for another is as capable of slander as thou art. I could go on but these few examples should suffice to make the point. Those maxims, grouped together, which have become our basic rules for good behavior, grew out of convenience, don't you see—man seeking to prolong his days while, at least, not worsening his circumstances, and by the simple ploy of treating his neighbors as he hoped they might see fit to treat him. Cynical, eh? No, no, eminently practical. Now do you see what logically follows?

"Well, for one thing, social living and the repression of man's atavistic instincts allowed more of the physically weak to survive. But unsuited to the life of warriors or hunters, alas, what was there for these fellows to do? Heretofore, such misfits had become priests or witch doctors or shamans. Well, to make a long story short, these new misfits became philosophers. And then, all to soon, became quite convincing as they preached against atavism and man living like the animals, claiming neither to be in harmony with the great principles that really uphold the universe.

"Eh? What principles? What is the first among them? 'Ah', they say, 'with our help man has discovered he has the potential to do what we uphold as good. What is more, he has the obligation to do this. Man must set his course to rise above his animal heritage and savage ways, the latter henceforth to be known as evil, for his spirit', say the philosophers, 'is inherently good. As the universe itself is inherently good. Thus man, if he is to find harmony, must subjugate his evil body to his noble soul. He must seek to live his days in goodness.'

"Well, there you have it, I believe. Good and evil both defined and their limits set. Philosophically.

"Meanwhile, what has happened to religion, however, while the philosophers have held their debates? Well, of course, you know who among the savages has charge of rites and rituals? The shaman, eh. And he, too, like as not, as we have seen, is a man ill-equipped to be a hunter or a fighter. Still he's a hardy old misfit and no slouch when it comes to cunning either. Accustomed as he is to dictate to his people in behavioral matters, he's not likely to let a bunch of upstart philosophers simply move in and take over. Them and their confounded notions of doing good. Hmph! One ought to be propitiating the gods as always. Sheer blasphemy! But, alas, blasphemy that cannot be dismissed.

"So what does he do, do you suppose? He assesses his adversary. He sees how the new scheme of things most directly threatens him. And he takes action.

"It chops at the very underpinnings of the traditional system, he remarks. In the old days individual gods were responsible for everything: all deaths, disasters and suffering, as well as what few blessings befell bewildered mankind. This new ethic of the good—apparently there is no hope of discrediting it—why not then embrace it? And to a startled world shamans united announce their discovery of the one true god, a single, omnipotent, creator god, who has not only made the universe but has seen fit to make it good.

"But why has this god waited so long to make himself known, people ask? Why, because only now have they been prepared to follow his ways. Only recently have the wise philosophers been able to formulate these ways. And, as the philosophers watch in dismay, their words are snatched from their lips, to become the creeds of new churches of Mithra, of Ormazd, of Amen-Re, of Quetzalcoatl, to name but a few. Not only have these wily shamans stolen the philosopher's powder but they've spiked his guns before making off with it.

"The role of the cunning old shaman in the development of modern religion, ladies and gentlemen, over-simplified and a bit abbreviated, to be sure, but there you have it. I use the generic term *shaman* because that term is archetypical. To some of you he may wear the robes of a prophet. In which case you may find it edifying to reappraise the history of the Isrealites, particularly that period prior to Abraham. In so doing you cannot fail to notice the emergence of one Yaweh from obscurity, to become Jehovah, the god of both Christians and Jews to this day.

"And now, for the sake of your notes, to recapitulate. Just where has this got us? Ah, yes. Very well, point one: a truly natural man, *id est*, one living without moral precepts, like any lesser animal, is an evil man, that is, by modern standards, religious or ethical, take your pick.

"Point two: man's first religions were evil religions—religions of evil, as it were—precisely because they were based on nature as man perceived it to be.

"Point three: the idea of the good, a philosophical formulation born of behavioral rules adopted by man perforce, as a result of social living, owes nothing to either nature or religion.

"Point four: religion, however, embraced the concept of the good; as a consequence, evolving the single, good, creator god.

"Point five: before the birth of the good creator god, religion served the function, and served it well, of giving man a sense of place in the natural order of things.

"By now I trust you are aware of some of the logical consequences of what we've said today. You can see, I assume, that the emphasis and direction of modern Christianity, as an example of a good, monotheistic religion, and those of Druidism, as an example of a religion rooted in nature, are rather opposite. Where one cherishes the flesh and pleads with the gods not to destroy it, the other insists it abhors this world and the flesh and begs its god to help the faithful through it; as quickly and as painlessly as possible, obliged as they are to remain here to prove themselves worthy of Heaven. Christianity, you see, is a man centered religion, viewing the universe through distinctly human eyes, even fantasizing about it. Druidism, on the other hand, like all valid ancient religions, starts with the universe as it is, the full weight of its vastness and mystery in tact, and, by establishing relationships with appropriate gods who control it, seeks to prevent that weight from crushing one. The direction is from the outside in, therefore, while the emphasis is not upon man at all but upon the whole of which man seems to be a scarcely significant part. Christianity, by minimizing the contributions of modern science, by relying so on Genesis and Revelations, at its worst oversimplifies the world. The world deserves to be mind-boggling, for indeed it is, which I think is about enough for today. I'm sure there must be questions. And I see we have a little time."

"Yessir," someone asked, "does what you say mean that Christianity is a false religion?"

"Ah, Mr. Dougherty, so it's you," said Professor Streghe. "Well, I knew that one of you would ask that question. Very well then. But now bear in mind that I'm commenting neither one way nor the other upon the teachings of Jesus, only upon organized Christianity, which term must be taken to include Rome, the Protestant churches and the various eastern offshoots as well. Agreed? Yes. Very good.

"Then insofar as organized Christianity is the product of human thinking and compromising, the work of many synods down through the centuries; insofar as there is no acceptable evidence that the universe was created whole and at once out of nothing, by any external agent, making the idea of a creator god an anomaly; insofar as the universe appears amoral, making man in harmony with it likewise amoral—well then, yes, Mr. Dougherty, organized Christianity is a false religion. Wait, but I have not finished, you see.

"Christianity also means a belief in the teachings of Jesus Christ. There is, however, the Christ, Who is the Son of God and the Messiah, and there is Jesus, the man from Nazareth, a carpenter, and much hangs upon how one confuses or distinguishes between the two. In any case, Mr. Dougherty, there seem to be as many interpretations as there are people to make them and we must wait until another time to get into any of them."

GENESIS

Frankly, I consider myself a bonafide heretic. That is, holding beliefs that, while they may have had their genesis in the womb of Christianity, grew to a mature form that Mother Church can only abhor. And/or condemn. Therefore, be warned. Everything I say must be considered suspect. Nevertheless, I want to address the question of how are we supposed to take the first book of the Bible, Genesis, the one that tells of Creation. Is it myth? Did the writer or writers think they were putting down fact? Did God Himself write it? Is it intentionally written as a sort of allegory?

First of all, no, I don't think God Himself wrote it. Enough said. I think men did and probably many of them. Perhaps over many generations. Until at last one man transcribed it all onto parchment, more or less in the form we know today. Except that it must have been in ancient Hebrew. So it had to come through Greek and Latin to get to us.

As to how much of it was originally thought to be factual and how much owed its present form to poetic license, I don't know. I suspect the people of the time when Genesis was written did believe that God actually made the world and all things in it in a finite amount of time. But just how much time they meant by a "day", who knows? Who really cares, anyway? Maybe a Holy Roller but I doubt if the Pope sits up nights worrying about it. And the Presiding Bishop of my old church probably gives it even less thought. So where are we then?

Regardless of how you interpret the word "day", as used in Genesis, men of biblical times believed that God made the world out of nothing and did so in a relatively short time. I'll bet you anything that's what they meant. The stars and the sun and the moon He placed in the dark sky. And then He made the earth and put it there, shaping seas and continents as He did so. Although people of that day probably had no real notion of continents. He caused the night and the day and made all the birds and fish and plants and animals to multiply and prosper after their fashion. To those ancient Hebrews, if it lived but didn't move, except in the wind, it was a plant. If it lived and moved over the ground, it was an animal. If it flew it was a bird. And the fact that it swam or lived in water made it some kind of fish. All this God made out of nothing but not man. Man was different.

God made the first man from a handful of already created dust, one of God's handfuls, to be sure, and then removed one of the first man's ribs, while poor Adam slept, and made from that a woman, Eve. The first man and woman, whose incestuous children seem to have spawned all the rest of us, were thus different from everything else. They were not made from nothing but of the material of the world itself and they were not made at all until everything else was in place and ready. Just what this says about us is anybody's guess. So don't mind me if I make one too.

Like a giant game of chess, Genesis seems to tell us, God conceived His world and the rules by which it was to be played. In six days He made the huge board and laid down the hard rules of nature. Then He put men upon the board to play the game. This seems to me to be the core of the story presented in Genesis.

The world is man's field of play and, while he must obey all its rules, he is given a freedom to play within those limits as he chooses. No other creature in God's world has that freedom. This also sets man apart. Of the world yet fashioned in the image of God Himself, man seems placed here to find his way back to the God Who loves him.

Of course, the ancient Hebrews never saw or heard of an ape. Nor had any idea that the first creatures rightfully to be called men probably appeared in Africa. They couldn't conceive of E=mc squared or envisage an earth rotating on its tilted axis as it revolved in elliptical orbit about the sun. To them night and day were ordained by God and, if days were longer in summer, it was God's wisdom that made them so. Summer was for planting and tending flocks and more daylight was a blessing. Winter nights were long because winter after all was a time of cold and waiting, best spent in a warm bed sleeping. They were not the beneficiaries of a great scientific enlightenment as we are today. But they were wise.

Many people have said that if they could have only two books to keep them company on a desert island where they had been cast up, their choices would be the works of Shakespeare and the Bible. I don't know. One of mine might be a good book on boat building, with and without tools.

MY GOD IS NOT DEAD . . .

SORRY ABOUT YOURS

For a while, when I was a lot younger, I thought of being a priest. Not the Roman Catholic Church but it's near cousin, the Protestant Episcopal Church of the U. S. A., offspring of the Anglican Church of the U. K. All of us have been young. Well, I was too. Once.

I was draining the very dregs of youth's despair one day when something hit me, striking to the depths of my youthful miseries and broke the dam that locked them there. It left me feeling refreshed and clean. That was the summer between my first and second years in college.

Now you may argue how much misery can a privileged kid be in, after all, especially on a sunlit beach at an exclusive resort in Long Island Sound, and I would answer, at the time, plenty. I was swamped with guilt and summer sunlight, and the privilege and the exclusivity of the island resort were probably no small part of it. What had I ever done, or would I do, to earn all this? How could I possibly deserve it?

So, if a silent cry of anguish directed at the clouds can be called a prayer, I prayed. And to feel so refreshed and clean came as my answer. It never occurred to me there might be a purely psychological explanation. I wouldn't know what to call it anyway. Thus, instead, I became convinced of both God and my call to His ministry.

But, alas, too soon that god died there in my gut. He took ill upon my return to school. Although I signed up to major in history, which a faculty advisor suggested would be a good choice for one going on to seminary, and otherwise prepared myself for my new life, late in my third year a worldly bishop spotted me for the fraud I was. Hardly a desirable candidate for ordination. Rather a fumbling, confused youth seeking solutions to his own problems. What the good bishop thought he saw was a troublemaker, if not a disappointment. Either I'd soon burn out, which he judged me to be in the process of doing before his eyes, or I'd flare someday in the pulpit, like a nova, only to scorch the dutiful around me. And the church had no place for hothead evangelists. Or burnouts either. In so many words, he told me, I just didn't have what it takes. There must be something else I could do.

By the time I went into the army it was clear to everyone I wasn't going on into the ministry. When I came out of the army I wasn't even going to church anymore. Dostoevsky and too much rubbing shoulders with the real world. Or too much study of comparative religions—I don't know—but I was permanently soured on the Christian Church as the institution that properly represented God upon Earth. I was also soured on the god that the Church purported to represent—Father, Son and Holy Ghost, some committee's notion of the living law of the universe, the result of much argument and compromise in many synods, called to arrive at an acceptable description of the fundamental axiom upon which rests the mathematical structure of the universe, that which resists the efforts of chaos to destroy the universe, and which lives in the hearts of men who seek truth. For in such terms was I coming to accept God. Not some entity defined and sanctioned by a human institution.

God is fundamental to reality, which rushes past us like costumed dancers at a masquerade ball, giving only glimpses of the passing dancers and making it all but impossible to determine the theme of the ball. It seems like a melee, not a parade. But if God is to reality as the theme we seek is to the parade we're watching, it's still not God Who created reality, any more than the theme can make the parade. Everyone in it makes the parade.

They don their costumes and take their places according to a plan, the object of which, if you see the whole thing, is to express some central idea, the theme of the parade of course—peace, movies are better than ever, the history of flight from Michelangelo to Mercury, whatever.

This theme, moreover, existed before the parade and will remain in memory long after the parade has passed. Succeeding parades on the same theme may differ in interpretation, according to their plans, but there will be no mistaking their indebtedness to the original. Each parade is an aspect of this theme, like a sculpture viewed from many angles. The universe is an aspect of reality and God is fundamental to reality.

God's real church is the human heart. And as there are upwards of how many billion human hearts beating upon this planet, there are undoubtedly as many Gods. But somehow, some day we'll find them all to be One. "In My Father's house are many mansions", Jesus is reported to have said. And I don't care which Jesus one listens to—Jesus the Galilean or Jesus the Christ and Son of God (I incline toward the former myself)—it's hard to interpret these words as meaning anything essentially but that God is the god of everybody, not just those who happen to agree upon some definition of His Nature.

Eventually the question for me became: did God create this universe or did He come into being with it? Indeed, was there ever any coming into being at all? Was there ever a void, in other words, a state of absolute nothingnesss? Or is this universe no work of creation but a manifestation, one of countless manifestations, of matter and energy as they dance their endless *pas de deux* across the stage of eternity?

My thinking along such lines began with what I called the Short Vector Theory. And what brought me to this was a couple of books: *The Brothers Karamazov*, for one, notably the chapter called The Grand Inquisitor. If you've never read it, the grand inquisitor has the actual Christ, on His second coming, locked up in the dungeon below, from whence, the inquisitor is explaining, he can never release the prisoner, although the inquisitor knows perfectly well Who Christ is; because Christ would proceed immediately to undo everything it has taken the church centuries to build and establish. The other book was by Neville Shute. Not *On the Beach* but *Around the Bend*, which underlines the fact that none of His gospelers actually knew Jesus and only one may have known the oldest of His twelve disciples, Bartholomew. If I'm wrong about this, so is a bishop and former teacher at the Virginia Theological Seminary. But the fact remains: no one knows what Jesus really said; only what He is said to have said. Do you know that party game in which one person whispers something in the ear of the person next to him, which that person passes on, and you see what you've got by the time it reaches the last person in the room?

I would never argue that Jesus never lived, nor died on a cross, anymore than I would deny the reality of Buddha, Confucius or Mohammed, but I question the supernatural role—the Son of God, born of a virgin, etc., etc.—just as I accept the possibility of grave robbers and reject the miracle of His physical resurrection.

And why not? In an age accustomed to miracles, what better way to launch a new religion than to claim an unheard of miracle? If it were not for fortuitous grave robbers, who may themselves have sought some miracle from His body . . . indeed I'm cynical enough to suppose the Christian religion founded upon an intentionally carried out hoax!

I realize now that even when I thought I believed, I had doubts. The Church was never for me. I may have thought so, even longed to believe in the Christian myth, which is quite beautiful, really, but something in me always resisted. The Church is for those who want their mysteries solved for them.

Thus, having been nurtured in the House of God, I came to look at it only from the outside. And began to permit myself the liberty of criticizing its architecture.

But, anyway, getting back to the Short Vector Theory, which went something like this: if you took a line as the zero degree base line, labeling one end of it positive and the other negative, and from the center point, called "the center of the universe", commenced to draw vectors representing all the forces in the universe—and I do mean everything: from love and hate to gravity and angular momentum—you would wind up, I said, with some vectors that extended in the same direction and added and some that extended in opposite directions and canceled each other, but you would have a whole bunch going in all different directions, like the spokes of a wheel. But these spokes would be of all different lengths, which in mathematical terms are magnitude.

However, by dropping perpendiculars from the points of each to the base line and adding and subtracting these shadows there, a resultant could be obtained, with a magnitude less than that of any single vector but a direction, positive or negative, representing the net effort of them all. This short vector, the resultant of all the vectors in the universe, is what I took to be God. I assumed its direction would be positive. Just as I assumed that all the individual vectors could be drawn correctly in the first place. Obviously a rash assumption but I was, as I said, a lot younger in those days. Now I'd be prone to say, instead of positive and negative, not even good and evil, but order and chaos. Still to take every vectorable quantity in the universe and to say to what degree precisely it contributes either to order or to chaos—I wouldn't be looking for God if I could do that, I would be He. Or at least the archangel Michael, I should think.

Ah, but wait a minute—are we talking about gods or do we mean God here? Gods have risen to prominence in every age with every culture. They are manifest in a people's need for them. They endure while their people endure, rise to power and decline alongside. Generally they reflect to a refined degree the character of the people over whom they preside. Zeus was a consummate Greek, as was Jupiter the most exemplary of Romans. Thus does Jehovah seem merciless and vengeful when the homeless Hebrews were struggling to survive in the many camps of their enemies. It was a time when charity was a luxury the children of Israel could scarcely afford.

Small wonder then that there sprang up among them the greatest messianic hope the world has ever known. Although it remains unsatisfied to the Jews, it is the origin of Christianity, which numerically at least, counting its Eastern, Roman Catholic and Protestant churches, has become the most espoused religion of the world.

But what do such numbers indicate? Unshakable faith? Conviction? I don't think so. One could count more true believers among the Jews, the Muslims, the Buddhists or the Hindus. How many Christians do you know who go to church for any number of reasons but conviction and faith?

Has the Christian God, therefore, as He did in my gut, sickened and died the world over? Over a century ago Nietzsche proclaimed Him dead. And in that time the world has seen and had to adjust to more unsettling changes than in the previous five hundred years.

Has God the power to cap the explosion of a nuclear bomb? Or save His people from the evil of a Hitler? Or halt the ravages of a disease like AIDS? It would appear not. If God ever had the power to intervene directly in the human sphere, then it would appear He has lost it.

The Old Testament of the Bible is full of accounts of miracles. And Christ is credited with performing them also. But the major miracles of the past thousand years or more have been the likes of appearances of the Virgin Mary to peasant girls. Pale by comparison to the sight of the Red Sea parting or of Joshua blowing down the walls of Jericho. Why have such miracles ceased to occur?

Well, of course, one explanation is that they never did. Rather they were an unsophisticated people's way of explaining things which they didn't understand. Rational, scientifically sound explanations have been proposed for the Red Sea's parting waters. But that leaves the question of how did Moses know? For that matter, how can the birds in the trees, even the leaves of the trees themselves, forecast a storm? On the other hand, the whole thing could have been the most fortuitous of coincidences. While a fissure in the ancient walls of Jericho could have vibrated and widened when assaulted by the trumpet blasts of the advancing Israelites.

According to Christian doctrine God intervened miraculously into human affairs to send His only Son into the world to reconcile His people with their God. But if God is alive and well and could still send His Son into this world, would He? Real faith in the Second Coming seems to be scarce these days. Those who profess to believe in it seem to be the least worldly and sophisticated among us? Snake handlers and holy rollers and such. Apparently, some natural affinity for miracles conveys upon a people's god the power to perform them. Is it harder, furthermore, "for a rich man to enter into the kingdom of heaven than for a camel to pass through the eye of a needle"? Taking rich in its broadest possible sense, to include a wealth of knowledge as well as skepticism, I think it must be. But could I accept and grow to love a God Who would reject me for using my mind? Somehow it reminds me of a bumper sticker I saw recently: "My God is not dead—sorry about yours." I just know the driver of that vehicle took the Bible to be literally true and accurate, despite mounting historical and scientific evidence to the contrary.

Whom Nietzsche proclaimed dead after all was the nineteenth century god of the European bourgeois. As indeed he is or should be.

If God, as Voltaire suggested He might be, is an invention of our own minds, then God must grow and prosper with us as a people. And wither and die as we do. Since the dawn of man many gods have died in fact. History records their obituaries: Ra, Zeus, Odin, Jupiter. We could name many more, associated with other peoples and places, from Sumer to Tenochtitlàn.

But certainly no god can be held accountable for so much as today he must. Reality has never been so grand nor so complex. Nor quite so threatening either. On a much smaller scale than God's, think of Jules Verne, who looked forward to rather than despaired of man's future. How naive he seems now. How would he have reacted to Hiroshima, do you suppose? Or to the Holocaust? While we simply take these horrors in stride and go on.

Do you think so many people visit the new Holocaust museum to suffer while they're being informed? Or do they go to be entertained? People are drawn to evil and fascinated by displays of it. And hypocrisy remains the one sin we all have a talent for. If God still lives, He may have turned His back on us.

In previous ages men had the decency, or the shame, to profess to be better than they were. I'm forced to think so, at any rate. The Victorians, for instance. While ours is called the Godless Age. But is it? Or do we need to set upon a new search for the one true God, Who has always been? Are there any signposts to show the way? Well, yes, I think there are.

Jesus, to be sure. I hesitate to say Christ for Christ is a title belonging to the Son of God, while Jesus was a teacher and a man. Like Buddha, I daresay. The great philosophical conflict between Buddhism and Christianity is over the self, which Christians think is both precious and inviolate. While Buddhists view it as a source of evil that must be denied. Buddha isn't a god at all, of course, but a prophet and a guide in the soul's rough journey through chaos to peace. But to a Buddhist his soul is universal. It is not his particularly and tailor made. While Christians take an opposite view. Basically Christians seem to confuse soul with self, to the point that they don't know which they mean when they say the other.

Regardless of whom you choose to be your prophet, though—
Jesus, Buddha, Mohammed or Confucius—all are monotheistic
in their thinking. And so am I. While my own notion of deity may
be more derived from Christian teaching, I confess to an
admiration for Tao. And I'm sure that a better student of the world's
religions than I have been could find traces of Buddhism in my
thinking. But, alas, the Hindus seem frankly pantheistic to me.
In any case, the role of the prophet is always the same—to relate
his people to his god. In both moral and religious terms. For God
relates to man that way. Religiously, obviously, but morally as
well. There are no atoms in the soul. The law that obtains there
must be a moral one.

And it goes without saying, Jesus, Mohammed, Confucius
and Buddha, cannot be the only ones. There are other prophets
or great teachers, writers or philosophers who have pointed the
way. Were one but to remind me of them, no doubt I would agree.
However, the task before us is not to plot the path but to define
the destination. Behind the veils upon veils between us and
ultimate truth, at the end of time and on the edge of space, God
waits untiring, somewhere in the farthermost fold of the final
dimension. Onward and upward, therefore, comrades, and may
truth be our reward!

Okay, having so stated our purpose, it would seem a good
idea at this point to lay down some parameters. Since we'll be
working toward a new definition of God, let's begin by reviewing
some of the older, more traditional concepts that we know we'll
be excluding from our definition. What God is not, in other words.

A. God is not the creator of the universe. If this universe of
which we are aware is not itself eternal, then the very stuff of it,
matter and energy, would seem to be. If one has trouble thinking
of matter as eternal, but rather something that must be created,
one has only to remember that any given quantity of matter,
multiplied by the square of the speed of light in unwarped space,
yields the amount of energy to which that mass can be converted.
Energy is not the sort of thing that one creates. Indeed that is in

one of the laws of thermodynamics, that energy can neither be created nor destroyed. And if there is energy, of which light is one form that seems to obey both the laws of quantum as well as wave mechanics, then mass upon mass of matter might be supposed to follow. Don't ask me how. Don't ask me about Entropy either. I confess I have never understood the latter concept very well.

But, anyway, was the Cosmic Egg, which blew up in the Big Bang, all the energy in the present universe but contained? Will this universe collapse someday? Shrink and compact itself into another strained glob of compressed hot energy? The penultimate black hole? And will this new cosmic egg finally split its seams, no longer able to contain itself, and fill some waiting void with another universe? I don't know. That's for God to know. For God is the engine and dynamic of this process, the laws by which it operates, not its maker but its governor.

I see but one God and one universe. But perhaps it is capable of configuring itself over and over again. And maybe even differently each time, seeking always to achieve perfect order. It may have tried this many times, many lifeless expansions and contractions, before allowing yet another of the endless embodiments of matter and energy to take shape and bring forth in its myriad forms life, of which each, except the ultimate, has been an experiment with but a single object: to achieve a form of life not only conscious of itself and its environment but bold enough and able to take hold of these and to seek to shape its own destiny. Meaning what exactly? Meaning choosing for itself to court order and to seek truth or to yield to chaos.

B. God is not the champion of good and enemy of evil. There is no good and evil. Instead there is order and chaos.

Nothing seems to me to be more ordered than a stable atom. One of the inert gasses comes to mind. They are an experiment in the search for order that succeeded. Not so complex as atoms to be found elsewhere on the Periodic Table but perfect and content to be left alone. They react with no other elements to produce compounds.

And on the cosmic scale don't we see this same striving for order? Are there not in our own system the so-called Main Sequence stars, which seem to be successful attempts at star building? They live orderly lives. While all around them we see the failures: stars destined to become Red Giants or White Dwarfs and die; glowing gas clouds still struggling to become stars; or the crazy misfits who destroy themselves, the Novae and Supernovae of the star world.

There are laws on the books of the universe that set forth the processes by which cosmic phenomena operate. Not only to exist but to do so orderly. Stars and stars that are suns with planetary systems and whole systems of stars called galaxies. No matter where we look, into the microcosm or out to the macrocosm, we see this evidence of order being sought. What we do not see, though, is the desire to rest and say, "There! The job is done." It's never done, apparently. Anything that works simply encourages the universe to try something bolder and more complex that may work as well. We see this in the valence bonding of complex atoms to form more complex molecules of compounds, in the coalescing of gaseous star stuff to form huge, swirling firmaments of stars, in the specific coalescing within these systems to form planets and moons about some stars and in the evolution of life upon our own tiny planet.

Order and progress. Order without progress yields stagnation. Progress without order leads to chaos. Chaos, of course, is the utter lack of order, plan or discipline, when chance rules supreme, when form becomes impossible and, therefore, everything disintegrates. Order, on the other hand, because it spawns both plan and discipline, makes form possible and lasting. By making form possible, order promotes progress. To say, then, that order seems good, while chaos seems bad, should be obvious.

Or to look at it another way. In human affairs the object of all good actions is to achieve or to maintain order. That is to promote social harmony, to preserve the unity of the family, to uphold the rights of the weak while not infringing too severely upon the needs of the strong, to protect the institution of marriage, etc., etc.. Would you not agree? Consider the Ten Commandments. If they were to be obeyed by every member of society, what an Eden would we find ourselves to be in! If order is the object of good, then order is what good men seek. To be good is not the end of the good life, therefore, but to achieve order. Good is the means to that end. And the opposite? Or disorder. Chaos indeed. That would be the end result if a means opposite to good were employed. Which is precisely how we define evil. Evil is the opposite, the antithesis of good.

God is not the champion of good either, for that is like making God the carpenter and not the architect. Good and evil are means. One leads to order. Perfect good to perfect order. The other leads to chaos. Death, disintegration, destruction.

C. God is not a person. Thus it is meaningless to talk of the character of God. God is like the ultimate mathematical formula. Without God the universe could not exist. It would have yielded to chaos and disintegrated.

But the universe does exist, and always it is striving to be more orderly. However, God does not see what God is doing. Nor care. In a lifeless universe God is unaware.

Yet, obviously, we don't live in a lifeless universe? How does God relate to us? If God is not aware, how can there be a relationship? Yet there is one and it's absolutely intimate. God in us, the Living God, as we shall see, is as vibrant and alive and aware as we are. More of this later.

D. God does not care nor intervene directly in human affairs. God, having no body, nor mind within that body, is powerless and remote. God is not aware of each of us. Nor all of us either, for that matter. God neither hears nor answers our prayers. All of these are true, I believe. It is God in us, the Living God, that knows us and sees us and is active in our affairs. We answer our own prayers and perform our own miracles.

So far so good then. We have some idea of what we don't mean when we say God. What do we suppose we do mean? Are we ready? Here we go.

A. In a lifeless universe God is the key to understanding it: how and why the universe works to achieve order while endlessly seeking to increase its own complexity. A kind of First Principle. I like to say the ultimate mathematical formula because words alone probably cannot describe God. In a lifeless universe God is no more aware of what's going on than is the binomial theorem when it's applied in the system known as Algebra. In the system of a single atom, God is like the force that binds the protons in the nucleus. We don't understand this force, can only hypothesize it in fact, but without it the atom would fly apart. There would be chaos and resultant destruction.

B. Life is not an accident. Nor the work of the hand of God either. Life is an exploration, a manifestation, of the endless possibilities of matter and energy. The thrust of life is to achieve intelligent life. Evolution works tirelessly in this direction. Evolution, once started, is like a chain reaction, an atomic pile feeding upon itself, moving inexorably in the direction of higher, ever more complicated, more adaptable life forms, until it achieves its goal. Evolution is relatively immune to the destructive inroads of chaos. Instinct, for instance, is inflexible—a very different force from free will.

C. Intelligent life, however, having free will, is at the mercy of chaos. And that which works in intelligent beings to thwart or supplant chaos, to restore and maintain order, is morality. And what is morality? Morality is the life force, the spirit of the living God. "The still, small voice" we hear sometimes. So what then is the Living God? He is God in us. The living God. The fundamental law of the universe, that seeks always to achieve and preserve order, given flesh and conscious choice. And the capacity to love, to care.

One can speak of the spirit of God now, the hand of God, the love of God, an act of God, etc., for God is now alive in us and shares our spirit and guides our hand. One can think of the Living God as a person too, just as we think of each of ourselves as a person.

And the relationship is symbiotic. That is, by co-existing in the same body, by cooperating, each experiences, man and God, life in a different dimension. For God, the eternal first principle, the uncaring, the unknowing, the rock upon which rests the awesome structure of the universe, there is living, there is consciousness, there is choice. For man, no less the beneficiary, there is direction, there is purpose, there is the perception of morality.

I believe in a moral universe. The man in whom the First Principle is most alive is a moral man. It's in the moral fiber of our being that God becomes alive.

For an intelligent life form, such as we are, morality is the working out of the First Principle. It is by living morally, observing fundamental rules, like the Golden Rule, that we build societies which truly benefit all their members. In other words, we establish and maintain order. But real order, not just lock-step conformity— real order that promotes real progress.

Any dictator can throw the fear of death and torture into his people and achieve a kind of order and, using them as slave labor, advance his ideas. But is this progress for mankind? No. Absolutely not. A deranged but brilliant monster like Hitler sets back the progress of mankind by a thousand years.

I do not mean we must live entirely for others either, but we cannot lose sight of them, in a headlong, endless blitzkrieg to reach our selfish goals. That is what happens in a world, or a part of it, ruled by chaos. Every man for himself and the devil take the hindmost. Tooth and claw. The law of the jungle, but the jungle is an orderly place by comparison.

I once heard a well-known writer, whom you never heard of probably, a descendant of Nathan Hale, nonetheless, say that the dedicated writer will let his mother mop floors to support them both, so that he, the artist, will have time to work; and if the money gets short and he can't afford ink, he'll milk her withered breasts and dye the milk black to carry on. She didn't say where he got the money for the dye or the paper.

I was impressed at the time, many years ago, but now it seems immoral. I don't think there was a great deal of the Living God sharing her body with Nancy Hale. Aym Rand again, did you say? Altruism and the selfish realization of personal ambition? I don't know, but the older I get, the more I think you have to try to strike some happy medium.

Well, so how do you know? How can you tell if your act is on track? Do you hear whistles and bells and cheers from on high? Or do you feel a quiet throbbing beat as your actions harmonize with the order of the stars? This is rather figuratively putting it but I think I would agree. Somehow amid the general noise and confusion of the universe we find the elusive sync pulses and lock onto them. The truth pulses. But tenuously. We are forever losing hold. The arm with which we reach for these is our soul, which I'd define as our divine conscience. Not our consciousness, as the Christian Church would allow us to believe.

And on that subject . . . no, I do not believe the persistent rumors that we pass through death still aware. When we die so dies our consciousness with us. But our thoughts and feelings conceivably, every tingle of our marvelous electrochemical brains, may go on forever, having tweaked the infinitely stretched energy fibers that bind our space. I don't know. But is that conscious survival of death?

I don't think so. Conscious survival of death is the coin with which the Christian Church buys its converts. Accept the faith, brother, and this gift shall be yours!

And on the subject of our divine consciences, our souls, if you prefer . . . the animals are born with instinct to guide them for they have no choice. While we who have the choice, at the heart of our incredible brains—indeed, it may be what we refer to as "heart"—we find a remarkable receiver. Like the instinct that guides the animals, it's pre-tuned to the heartbeats of eternal truth. It is in fact the "heart" of the Living God within us, its beat the sync pulses that steer us to the better of choices, the best of paths. They are weak, however, these beats, and we do drift off. And chaos crowds in. But the receiver remains alive to try to get us back.

There may be people, though, in whom this receiver never functions, damned people in whom God can never exist. Their receivers may be drowned or crushed by all the chaos in their lives. There may be real psychopaths, in other words—men and women, even children who have no moral sense at all.

By the same token, there may be times when the output of this receiver, usually feeble, fairly booms in us, as when in some circumstances we develop a passion for justice. Justice now, not revenge. We have a natural desire for justice, most of us, which is only an expression of our moral yearning in the first place.

Passion, though, is unbridled, difficult if not impossible to control. Like starved horses turned loose in the oats field. If this were the condition of the universe, there would be chaos. Thus, the heart in which God lives is compassionate. And quietly courageous. The mind that God shares is wise. Jesus is a perfect example.

Not without reason are we told the stories of the fig tree and the casting out of the money changers from the temple. These are both cases where Jesus yielded to passion. As He did upon the cross when He asked why God had forsaken Him. They are contrasts with His more exemplary behavior. They are meant to show His human frailty. Jesus was a man but a man who understood the fundamental truth of God and the relationship of that truth to humanity.

Passion is one of our excesses. Not necessarily bad but to be guarded against and allowed only infrequent free rein. But passion is cathartic. It is also catalytic. Many times acts of which we might seem incapable we commit in "a fit of passion". These can be good and laudable as well as evil and depraved.

Yes, if it were not for intelligent life, God would indeed be the ultimate mathematical formulation of the universe. Passionless, in fact, unfeeling. Something like that. But man gives God other dimensions. There exists between man and God a symbiotic relationship in that, without God's moral direction, man cannot hope to realize himself, or achieve his destiny, while God without man is in no sense a living god. When the consciousness of man becomes the consciousness of God, then God is alive. And that is the Living God. And so long as God lives the universe is a moral one, for morality is the working out in human terms of the eternal First Principle that guides the universe, through order, toward progress. The search for truth, therefore, is a moral one, indeed a moral obligation. While perfection? Who knows? Chaos, too, seems to be woven into the fabric of the universe. And then, to be sure, there's that damned entropy, which I confess again I don't understand.

Enough, enough! But what is the destiny of man? Would you know what I meant if I said the destiny of man was to become God? The universe is to be understood, you see. But God, since God did not make it, cannot understand it. God only governs. God is like Robert's Rules of Order in this respect. God can outline how a member is to be ousted from the body politic but God cannot physically remove him. That power belongs to the Sergeant at Arms, having been conferred upon the latter by the rules. God in one's heart gives a man power he could never have otherwise. But God alone in a lifeless universe is powerless. And unknowing.

Imagine a two dimensional universe in which there exist shadow-like sentient creatures without height, who are aware that they draw dotted lines on the beach wherever they walk. (Now cut me a little slack on this; I'm perfectly aware that footprints have depth). But they've yet to tie these lines together into geometric shapes, such as squares and circles and triangles. Okay?

Now. Unprovable in their own terms—*a priori*—for, in effect, they define their terms, there also exist a host of propositions regarding these undiscovered shapes: the Pythagorean theorem, for example. To these child-like and unsophisticated creatures, who have not realized what purpose may lie in their aimless strolls upon the beach, the Pythagorean theorem, which they lack the knowledge and ability to state even, may seem to one of them the very voice of God one day when it states itself in his head, after countless measurements and playing with these odd three-sided shapes as yet unnamed as triangles.

We, too, are child-like and unsophisticated, in this universe we call our home. And God is unknowable, because neither have we discovered all the shapes there are. So, too, in us is the Living God a child. Man and God, the symbiotic pair, must grow together and investigate all until the gap between sentient life and the unknowable has been bridged, until there is one mind in the universe that knows all and itself as well.

Not a bad destiny, eh? One's destiny, after all, is a goal which one is particularly shaped to achieve, which no one else can hope to achieve. There is no guarantee that the goal will be achieved. Indeed, there is none that it is achievable. We know only that it is reserved for us. But what would happen if it were achieved?

Then does it all start over: a new universe, a new sentient life form? How long will it take this time? Or maybe man is not alone in this universe. Who knows?

I surely don't. I don't pretend to know why good men are struck down while, right beside them, evil men continue to prosper. And escape the consequences of their deeds. But if asked I would say chaos. I don't know anything but I suspect that there's a purpose in life. And that purpose is to seek God and truth. Which is the same thing, really. We long for answers to all our questions while, within us, the child-like Living God seeks communion with his blind and deaf and dumb Father.

That's one way to look at it. Another is to say that since Man has conceived of God, if Man has a destiny, it may be to become God.

THE CHRISTIAN CHURCH:

MAN'S OR GOD'S

At the risk of boring you I want to come at this one last time. I've mentioned Dostoevsky. Well, like him, I've wrestled with Christianity all my life. Of course at first I didn't fight it. I was just a kid. I accepted and tried to believe. My doubts didn't take hold until I was in my twenties. But even as a child I hated Sundays. And the only things I ever really liked about church or the services were the Christmas and Easter hymns. The rest I simply assumed as part of my burden for being who I was and for being headed in the direction everybody seemed to agree I should be going.

Frankly, as a pre-adolescent, I was hardly capable of such incisive analysis. Alas, hindsight far exceeds the acuity of first exposure.

Anyway, I saw this church going up not long ago. It was in Houston and it was just a steel skeleton like hundreds of others in that sprawling city where most such structures turn out to be stores or office buildings or condo dwelling units. But what immediately identified this as a church was the fully fabricated and painted steeple already set in place atop it. And from the design of that steeple it was apparent that the church itself would be of neo-classic persuasion. No doubt brick veneer would be pasted hastily to its steel and gypsum walls.

Ah, well, get it up in a hurry, I thought. The American way. God may have patience but we surely do not. But then God has all eternity to wait in. What were scores and scores of years to God to see the gothic splendor of Notre Dame finally realized? Nor did people then take such notice of the passage of time. They began the cathedral in the twelfth century to finish it sometime in the thirteenth. A hundred years! But life in the Middle Ages consisted of toil and poverty in the shadow of ignorance, highlighted fitfully by the nobles who made frequent war; while Mother Church held out the promise of immortality in Paradise but first you had to die. When life offers so little in the living, patience becomes a necessity. Furthermore, the Church had the power to make men embrace it, or fear it, since it reserved the right to deny men Paradise, to plunge them instead into eternal damnation.

Today, however, the most ignorant American knows that his kind have walked on the Moon. While what he has gleaned from just the pictures in comic books would confound the likes of Copernicus. How does the Church address itself to a populace so sophisticated? What has the Church become to survive in the twentieth century?

During the first half millennium the Church, founded by Christ on the rock of St. Peter, sought mainly to expand. During the reign of the Roman emperor Constantine, Christendom spread to cover not only the Middle East and the African shores of the Mediterranean but most of what we know as Europe and Asia Minor today. And Rome became the heart of the body of Christ on Earth. Then during the fifth and sixth centuries Europe was overrun by barbarians. The Gauls, the Goths, the Visigoths and the Vandals. None of whom had any love for books and learning and heartily no desire to be Christians! The Church was thrown on the defensive, retrenching. No longer was it possible to expand.

So the Church appointed itself the guardian of knowledge. It survived by safekeeping to offer the world the one thing at some point it must have—knowledge. But it also grew powerful. For a thousand years monks built libraries by copying the few circulating books by hand. During the Dark Ages their candles as they worked were the only steady light. And then the Renaissance changed all that.

In the beginning, during the innocence of its own youth, the Church had been the sower of the Word, the disseminator of the Good News of Christ. And what made the news so welcome was the promise of Paradise. At last a man had a reason to endure all his sufferings. What enabled the early Church to grow as it did was that so many desired its prize. Its exclusive prize, I might add, for the Church denied the right of any rival to offer it. And Christians became so many they could not be ignored; so desperate they could not be discouraged. Rome tried persecution and it failed.

Still no empire can endure without the willingness of its subjects, no matter how grudgingly that willingness may express itself. And Rome was no exception. Already crossing swords with the barbarians on its frontiers, Rome accepted what seemed to be becoming the religion of its interior provinces simply to save itself. Christians did not seem to hold their lives so dearly that they would never risk them to achieve real freedom. And an enemy in front is only strengthened if there is also an enemy behind one. Thus, from the time of Constantine until Rome itself was sacked, Christianity became the official religion of the emperors and the empire and the Holy Roman Catholic Church became the official spokesman for God in this world. There was only a real challenge from the Eastern Orthodox Churches, which recognized their pope in Constantinople as the only true head of the faithful. These churches had grown out of a series of schisms between Constantinople and Rome. Constantinople was the political capital of the Eastern Empire while Rome ruled the west. Meanwhile, the Roman church knew no other serious rival until the Reformation, when the marital fickleness of an English king brought into being the Anglican Church of England and its offshoot, the Episcopal Church in America that we're familiar with today.

Of course the Reformation also put the word "protestant" into common usage. Since it there have been Lutherans, Methodists, Presbyterians and Baptists, to name but a few, with the result that the Church, by which term let us now include the Protestant as well as the Catholic churches (I don't feel qualified to speak for Eastern Orthodox Christians), grew to cover the entire known world. What changes do we see in this institution, then, during the last five hundred years? Do we see any modifications of its basic objectives?

Well, for one thing, once the Church had achieved this organization that spanned the civilized world, it entrenched. Time enough to convert the remaining heathens later. It would put its own house in order first. It realized what power was within its grasp, what power in fact it already had. It never gave up missionary work entirely but strengthening and improving the organization, without regard to spreading the faith, became an end in itself. Study the history of the Vatican. The protestant churches, although they may seem more democratic, are no less bureaucratic.

Gone of course were the zealots who'd carried the Word from Palestine to Canterbury, from Madrid to the New World. No need for their emulators at this point. On stage came the business-like professionals, serving Christ as a career, who made out efficiency reports on each other, who sought the material rewards of any other career. The Church became concerned with budgets and finances and salaries and the Good News it once gave away became the top of the line it offered for sale. The eye of the needle opened and rich men lined up to pass through it. The Church found itself fabulously wealthy. And those blessed to have a place in its ranks shared in this wealth accordingly. With Original Sin the corner stone of its advertising campaign . . .

Original Sin. What a clever doctrine that is. At once absolving us of guilt for being bad while at the same time threatening to punish us regardless. We can't help being rotten; we were born that way; but Hell still waits for those who choose to ignore God's forgiveness, while they yet live in this world. Thanks to Original Sin the Church had no trouble selling its full line of panaceas for guilt and fear.

The Church practically pioneered religious marketing. And to see just how successful that's become one has only to turn on the television or the radio and tune in one of the "electronic evangelists" so popular today. The Church by its example taught them all they know.

Radio and television audiences include many of the frightened and the guilty, as you know, many of the crippled and the bedridden and the ill. "Brothers and sisters, send me your dollars," says the electronic evangelist, "and I will pray for you." And they do. They're gullible, alas, and many of them are ignorant. They believe the man will pray for them and I'm sure he does. Their mistake is in thinking that his prayers should sound louder in God's ear than their own. But this is exactly what the electronic evangelist counts upon most heavily. He may even believe it himself, for all I know.

Knowledge may foster doubt but ignorance surely does fear. And fear gives these fellows their other good shot at the poor folks at home. Many of whom are scared clear out of their wits by conditions in the world today. To these science has made the world seem godless and incomprehensible. They feel torn up by the roots, blown through trackless deserts by random winds and many hear the rumble of Armageddon beyond the dunes. Into the intellectual vacuum of their minds the electronic evangelist pours his palliating fundamentalism and the dried sponges of their wind seared souls soak it up. "Away with doubts and fears," says the electronic evangelist. "Brothers and sisters, believe! Send in your dimes and dollars and Paradise shall be yours!" And the people open their starved hearts to his words even as they open their purses to the preacher.

We've all seen and heard these fellows. Under tents. On the radio or on the tube. Some preach and some harangue. Some heal and some come on like intellectuals, calling attention to their mid-west Bible school D. D.'s. But there's not one of them who appears to have made any such sacrifice as he calls upon his listeners to make. To the contrary, they must pay hundreds of dollars for their suits. And they stuff silk handkerchiefs in their breast pockets. But don't give them credit alone for their vanities. The pattern was set for them centuries ago when the Church first realized what a good thing it had. SALVATION FOR SALE! FORGIVENESS OF YOUR SINS! AT A PRICE TO SUIT ANY BUDGET! WE TAKE AMERICAN EXPRESS, VISA & MASTERCARD! Like other hawkers of the day, why didn't they just go ahead and put up the signs?

There is one great difference between what these modern charlatans, the electronic evangelists, seem to do, however, and the way the Church itself conducted business. There's still a whole line of goods those guys can't really peddle. The Sacraments. The Church's answer to the needs of our lives from the cradle to the grave and beyond: Baptism, Marriage, Holy Communion or the Mass, Extreme Unction, etc., etc. There are seven of these sacraments and only a priest, Roman Catholic or protestant, who stands lawfully in the Apostolic Succession from Peter on down, by the Laying on of Hands, can administer them. Baptism and marriage are exceptions. But, make no mistake, for one coin or another they are all for sale.

There is also a huge market the electronic evangelist can't hope to penetrate. Today the world is very sophisticated compared to half a millennium ago. For everyone today who might welcome the electronic evangelist into his heart there are two who will shut him out. His mixture of pap and brimstone is for simpletons, they insist. The poor, the sick, the ignorant and the downtrodden. Not for them. They're emancipated. Yet between the hours of ten and twelve on Sunday mornings many of these very people will flock to churches in their neighborhoods. Why? Is the Church's presentation of essentially the same merchandise so much slicker it gets past their cynicism? What distinguishes these people from the spiritual pap-slurpers they're so ready to pity as fools?

One glimpse of the parking lot will tell you. Do you see any old cars? They're nearly all successful people. Successful people generally don't do things not calculated to make them more successful. That's why they go to church. Oh, they may tell themselves otherwise and go through the motions of seeking salvation and praying for the forgiveness of their sins but in all probability what they really want for their patronage is respectability. They want to come to the attention of the better people in their community, whom they assume will be there. The least selfish thing they want is for their kids. Like all of us, they worry about their kids on the streets. And the Church offers a decent environment as well as wholesome activities for young people of all ages. Terrific. Go to church and gain respectability, which can't hurt you in your business or career, plus find varying degrees of help in the difficult job of parenting, which many of us feel so unequal to these days.

So the Church has become a kind of club for its adult attendants while it offers itself as a community center for their offspring. And the sophisticated modern priest or pastor, preaching from his Sunday pulpit, doesn't harp on the wages of sin and the life everlasting, as he might have done in more innocent times—no, he slides all that to the back burner, keeping it handy but what he cooks up front for his congregation are savory sermons seasoned with practical morality. His emphasis is on the good life and the here and now. Nor is he any more dedicated to the saving of souls than he should be. The Church has broken into a new market and he is first and foremost a salesman. What sells now must appeal to successful businessmen and professionals. They don't want to think about the next world. They've got all they can handle in this one.

So, must we conclude that all clerics have become as worldly as their flocks. No, of course not. Most do believe in God, I'm sure. And most do try honestly to live helpful lives. Yet my own experience with clergymen, most of whom have been Episcopalians, is that when it comes to saving souls they tend to concentrate on the easy marks. Perhaps because they must. Like other salesmen, they have their quotas, so to speak. If they wish to advance in their own ranks, or reap greater rewards where they are, they must show themselves to be successful. But there is so much else they must attend to first. They just don't have the time to talk at length with anybody. And it takes time to overcome a person's doubts and fears. The business of the modern church in their hands is too demanding. While individual clerics may wish things were otherwise, it's the fault of the system in which they must operate. Pack 'em in and keep 'em happy is the way to do it today. And the stray lambs that slip away, let 'em go. There isn't time to chase them anyway.

The arrival of the twenty-first century will mean that the Church has survived for two thousand years. And it means to survive for thousands more. It has survived so far by keeping a close eye on us, adapting to our changing mores. It hasn't had to do much to accommodate itself to our changing nature. We are the same upright apes who forsook the trees. In fact, all the Church has had to do to keep step with us is to update its product line and to refurbish its ad campaigns so they remain appealing to us as we become more and more sophisticated. By offering to sell us in every age what we do not think we can provide for ourselves— namely, escape from our nagging, sometimes torturing, guilt and erasure of the fear of death—the Church still seeks to increase its wealth and power over us. Just as in the Middle Ages the Church found power in knowledge, so too has it learned that with wealth there comes even greater power.

Power is what the Church seeks. Not military or political or economic power specifically —well, not lately at any rate, but there have been both war-like and loving popes in Rome since Peter was crucified and succeeded—spiritual power is what the Church thrives on. The power to manipulate men's souls. And, by so doing, their consciences, their hopes, their dreams, their greeds and ambitions, their fears and dreads and everything else as well. For power not exercised will atrophy and shrivel, just like muscle tissue. Speaking of which, let me liken the priesthood, the clergy, to the muscle tissue of the Body of Christ on Earth. Although the Church accomplishes everything through them, the clergy individually are not to be blamed for all the institution's practices. They're by and large good men but they're like cells, like the cells of our bodies which are individually alive and can reproduce. But the living body has the dominant agenda. The Church too is alive as a body. It has a corporate brain and a nervous system. And the clergy are as subject to the directives of that brain, to the reactions of that nervous system, involuntary some of them, as the muscles of my body or yours are to our brains and nervous systems. Even the Pope.

If the Church was ever God's House in this world, and we the weary travelers seeking rest and refreshment, but not able always to pay, the ambitions of men soon drove God out of it. The true House of God is each human heart. The Living God is within us. And what passes for God in the churches is as surely man-made as Baal, the false god of the Old Testament.

THOUGHTS

For a dictionary:

Scuzz—stain, deposit or discernable effect on a subject material, liquid or solid, as a result of exposure to a polluted environment. The adjective form would be *scuzzy*.
Useful expressions such as "all scuzzied up" are also practical.

To describe being shot in the head:

A flash of crimson blinded him, coincidentally with the first clap of a deafening roar of thunder, the rest of which he never heard.

Politics and goodness:

Politicians are given goodness like drops in a bottle. If not used it will evaporate anyway. Some works of theirs, which they may wish to endow with goodness, will be like stainless steel, however—no more lastingly marked by good intentions than by bad.

People who live in glass houses:

It is so popular to say that people are "no damn good" but such critics never seem to include themselves in their condemnation.

Personal property:

The only thing that makes anything truly yours in this world is if all those to whom you might be beholden for it are dead, or if you won or achieved or purchased the thing with your own resources alone.

Character depiction in a story:

People are shaped by their environment just as surely as they are colored by their genes. When one sets out to write a story one is setting up an entire environment. If any of the story flowing from one's hand is not a faithful reproduction of observed life, therefore, some of the environment constituted by the story will be imagined. Right? Thus, it is not a good idea to copy one's characters too closely from living people. They may not quite fit the environment in which they must find themselves in the story.

Prayer:

What is prayer? Prayer is a supplication. One is asking something of God. But if God is to hear there must first be communication. Therefore, prayer is an attempt to communicate with God. So Who or What is God and what constitutes an attempt to communicate with Him or Her or It? Whatever it is, that's a prayer.

Death:

Is it no peace of mind at the end to think that all you've thought and felt has become as ripples spreading across the limitless pond of space and time? In that sense *you* personally *may be* eternal.

A CREED FOR THE

MILLENNIUM

I think we all need to believe in a higher power greater than ourselves. In our hearts we know we can't be trusted to be entirely in control of everything. And the responsibility would be shattering if we were.

Even if that higher power is but the blind, instinctual struggle of the universe to achieve order, in spite of rampant chaos, we need to believe.

For me that instinct *is* God.

I believe in God, Which did not make the universe nor can undo it, but Which is one with it, the truth of Which shall outlive the universe and remain, as eternal as Energy itself. If the universe is evolving, therefore, God is evolving with it. However, if the universe is but grand evidence of an evolving Reality, then God is the first reality. If I must think of God as a creator, I think of God as having made Energy. And turned it loose. Perhaps God could not hold it. And of having made Time, too, perhaps as a way of controlling Energy, some kind of limit at least. But I cannot think of God as a person.

I believe that God's name is best spelled in symbols of some mathematical nature, symbols of some high math yet unknown to us. God is the ultimate formula from which derives all order in the universe. God is not alive yet lives in us. I believe that God can have no life without us, no more than the stars themselves can be said to be alive. We are the evidence of the Living God and from the Living God does all order in our lives derive. We are neither God's servants nor His children, though, and I cannot accept that we are God's creations. We are the products of evolution. But it is our peculiar destiny to spell God's name. We have the potential to become God. We, or a higher form of us, in some universe more perfected than this one. Morality in our lives, therefore, confused though it may become, derives from the Living God. Ultimate morality may be said to be His voice. It is to the sound of His voice that we should tune the ears of our hearts.

It is a symbiotic relationship, in other words, ours with God. We give God life; He gives us order. But along with God there exists Chaos. And Energy may be said to know no master. All we see derives from Energy and is powered by it. But all we see is not order. Nor is there much in our own wild lives. Look at history. There we see a struggle going on, as old as Time itself, the participants being Order and Chaos. And perhaps winning is not the point but, rather, to achieve some balance. No balance can be permanent, however. There is no standing still.

I was born into a Christian home and baptized in a protestant church. But of Jesus Christ I must say I do not believe in his divinity. He among western world prophets, if not among all prophets, was the one man who best understood God, I believe, and thus the one man in whom the Living God was most alive. It is unfortunate that all the teachings of Jesus Christ we have, we have at best but second hand.

INDIAN LIFE

If life can be defined as an organismic process characterized by metabolism and growth, observable reaction to stimuli and the capability of reproduction, and if the overseer of this process, that which judges its myriad forms to be successes or failures, and either tolerates or replaces them—there being no allowance made for effort alone, as is the case in our schools commonly—if this overseer is none other than the discovery of Charles Darwin which he called Evolution, then the foregoing might be considered to be a fairly accurate description of the scientific view of life. Yes, of course. But not the American Indian's, however.

I have just been reading my first Frank Waters novel, this one THE WOMAN AT OTOWI CROSSING, in which he pretty much lays out the Indian view of life, at least that of Indians of the American southwest. And I find it strikingly Buddhist.

Like the Buddhist the American Indian, according to Waters, seeks release from the limitations and confines of his individual selfhood. And to become one with the timeless oneness of reality. The Indian's view of time is not the same as that of a scientifically oriented white man, however. As Waters puts it: ". . . to Indians time has depth instead of movement. Like a great, still pool with a life and meaning of its own. As if it were an organic element which helps to fashion our own shape and growth in its unique design of being. Indians aren't in any hurry; they have all the time there is."

I'm not quite sure what that means. But one thing seems clear. The Indian, who may have an ingrained sense of his soul's journey through whatever realms of being he may envisage, seems to have very little or absolutely no sense of any ordained purpose of his being. Other than to complete this journey if he can. He seems to have no sense of man's destiny, for instance, of what it is he is supposed to do, having found himself apparently alone on tiny Earth, practically lost among the millions and billions of visible and invisible stars. He does not believe in evolution. All creatures, himself included, came into the world in just such form as he sees them himself. And he looks for no change in these forms. They are eternal. He looks for no change in the world, either. The universe is as it has always been. And will always remain. Time is "a great, still pool", did not Waters say?

Naturally, the Indian in arriving at these convictions did so without benefit of modern scientific investigation. He made no study of fossil remains. He has carbon dated nothing. He had no telescope when he contemplated the heavens.

Nor did Siddhartha Gautama, the Buddha, twenty-five hundred years ago when he experienced his "Great enlightenment", under the East-Indian bo tree, and subsequently preached the sermon that contains the gist of Buddhism to this day. The Buddha did not have benefit of scientific studies and equipment either. He too accepted the universe as is and thought it permanent. Our perception thereof, at any rate. At least, to my understanding of Buddhist thinking, he did. The world, therefore, is unchanging. And men must seek detachment from it and, eventually, through a series of lives, achieve total release from self and all selfish concerns. Ideal anonymity, I suppose, as well as loss of the awareness of oneself, but, at the same time, oneness with what is truly real, which for that very reason is quite indescribable. Man can only see the illusions of his senses, to which are added the imaginings of his brain. A quantum physicist might tell you the same thing. A rock is not as you perceive it. It's something else altogether. An organization of atoms which absorbs certain frequencies of light energy and reflects others.

This attitude toward self, though—self awareness, self consciousness, self preservation, self indulgence, individualism generally—seems to be common to both the East Indian Buddhist and the North American Indian alike. The American Indian, however, being perhaps the less strict in its application. The absence of a sense of racial destiny or mission, each man doing his part as best he can, seems characteristic of both also.

One might say at this point that it is the Christian religion, five hundred years younger than Buddhism, that builds its doctrines upon the twin corner stones of these very rocks that the Buddhist and the American Indian refuse: self and racial responsibility. And need I say here that I am not using the word *race* to mean red, black, brown , white or yellow but as in the race of man. It is Christianity that glorifies self to the point that the true Christian expects to find himself, still aware, in the presence of God in Heaven, as his reward for having lived a good life.

What's more, all men, according to Christian doctrine, Christian and heathen alike, bear the responsibility for man's original sin, that of denying God by an unheard of act of deliberate disobedience. Thus it becomes the mission of all men, Christian and heathen alike–hence, mankind–to earn absolution of this sin and, thereafter, by leading an exemplary life of good works and self-sacrifice, to gain entrance to Heaven.

I don't mean to pursue this any further. It's obvious that such thinking should find little welcome in the house of a dedicated Buddhist. Or in the hogan of a typical unrepentant American Indian. The fact that Europeans were so successful in converting the Indians owes much to the Roman Catholic Church's devotion to statuary, holy symbols and icons, as well as the poetic beauty of biblical stories themselves. Few indeed were the converts who truly understood the church's theology.

So what happened in the world in the five hundred years since the birth of Buddhism to explain the radical shifts taken by Christianity? The Greeks probably. The whole Mediterranean world, thanks to the Romans, fell heir to the thinking of the Greeks. While the Greeks in their own time, plying the waters of the Inland Sea, had already changed that part of the world forever.

The Greeks glorified man. Their gods were in the image of man. And the Greeks worshiped heros, in other words, stand-out individuals. Their heros became gods. Often they were half gods to begin with. Would the Arabs have allowed Lawrence to lead them against the Turks had the Greeks never been?

The Greeks, of course, never sailed through the strait of Gibraltar. Not that we know of. They never knew India, China, Japan were even there. Nor did the Romans. And therein may lie a tale.

First the Romans gave into Christianity. And then Europe in its entirety became Christianized. The Middle Ages entrenched Christianity still further. Then came the Renaissance and the birth of modern science and there was no way that western man was going to embrace Buddhism in any large numbers.

There are American Buddhists, to be sure. Many of them. It is the selflessness, Karma, reincarnation and the ultimate reward that follows total renunciation of self and all its trimmings, and with self the loss of awareness too, obviously—anonymity that is as absolute as it is mindless—the ultimate reward of oneness with . . . With what? Waters calls it the "one great unity of all creation." The Buddha himself said it was indescribable.

Anyway, it is to be free of the baggage of self, to be free of responsibility, actually, and to be free of the nagging sense that one must do something in this world to justify one's presence in it.

There are no free lunches, as the saying goes. And the gift of life isn't free either. Not to all, apparently. Unless you're an American Indian. And then it comes as free to you as it does to a deer or a bird or a frog. Two very, very different ways of thinking.

And the American Indian may have brought his with him when, as modern anthropology tells us, he crossed the Bering Straits land bridge to get here from Asia.

Buddhism may be an Asian thing after all, as inevitable in the thinking of the East Indian as death itself. It is death that makes us religious anyway, you know. "There are no atheists in the foxholes", was a favorite saying of World War Two.

Two ways of thinking about the same reality and who's to say who's right? I feel compelled to follow self, myself, accept evolution and responsibility and to pursue my personal destiny as a card-carrying member of the human race. If the American Indian or the Buddhist doesn't see it that way I still wouldn't refuse to buy either a beer.

MEXICAN WOMANHOOD

If Maria Felix, now in her seventies, personifies the passionate, indomitable character of Mexican women, quick to joy or anger and as fiercely jealous as they can be courageous, Dolores Del Rio, now deceased, does the honors for the other side of the coin. On this the complementary side we see a face long-suffering but proud, a woman who stands ready to mother and love her family at the total expense of herself, who expects from life more grief than happiness but whose eyes never grow old, only wiser. Both women, of course, are beautiful. Mexico boasts some of the most beautiful women in the world, actually.

Another interesting thing one notices when comparing these two women, taking notes while studying the roles they have played, is that Maria Felix seems so often a man in woman's guise. There is about her a masculine directness, a forthright courage, and of course her deep-toned voice, but the engine that drives her is female. Her passion is a woman's passion. For all her confrontational directness, it is not logic and reason but her heart that impels her to the brink.

Dolores Del Rio, on the other hand, in her films is typically somebody's mother, or, if not, she is a loving woman who most certainly deserves to be a mother. Dolores Del Rio is as female as female can be. Her voice is soft, her eyes full of wonderful sadness, and if circumstances compel in some role she plays, and she must lash out at another character, one can see the pain it costs her written on her face. By contrast Maria Felix's dark eyes flash with fire and she exults in her power when she blows righteous steam.

Dolores Del Rio is a woman forever seeking true love who is willing to give more than she gets to win it. Maria Felix is looking for a man who is not in awe of her. Not one who will beat her— nothing so crude—but a man who can stand up to her, lock eyes with her and stare her down at last. It is her character that must be met head on and dominated, not her body. Her body remains a free animal thing that must never know either leash or cage.

There flows in Maria Felix the blood of the Moors, the hot, proud, ruthless blood of Spaniards who spawned and supported the Inquisition, mixed in Mexico with the strong red blood of the stoic and indomitable Indians. The heart of Dolores Del Rio pumped her arteries full, too, with these same rich juices, but there must have been the admixture of something more refined. Not simply that she seemed more ladylike, carried herself with such inherent dignity, but the capacity she seemed to have to suffer. And yet not be destroyed by it. The French perhaps. Jeanne d'Arc comes to mind.

In these two women I think one sees epitomized, isolated and tagged as if the results of a laboratory analysis, the traits of character that in differing proportions and to differing degrees identify the best of women in Mexico today.

THE SECOND WORLD

One thing that bothers me . . . well, of course, many things bother me—living mothers-in-law, dying roses—and this is not one of the things that bothers me most either. But it ranks right up there with a mosquito bite. We hear so much about the poor retarded Third World, so far behind us who must be presumed to live in the First World, that one wonders—at least, I do—who, what, where do we look to find the Second World? I don't know. Yet there must be one. If there weren't, the Third World would be it, would it not? What did we skip when we jumped from one to three? What is there about the Second World that it must remain so hidden that few indeed even dream it exists?

Things must be better there than they are in the Third World, yet not so good as we experience them to be here in the First. It is, after all, the Second World we are talking about. It must be where people live who are too educated and capable to be typical of the Third, yet still not able to cut it in the First. Is it a transition world then? Like Roman Catholic Purgatory, we spend time there until we've earned the right to go on to Heaven? Again, I don't know. But it seems to me that if this Second World is some kind of transition place, there must be in it the means by which one can get oneself out of it. Don't you think? Like schools? Do I mean schools? God, at this point, I wish I knew. I've never even seen the place, nor do I have any cherished expectation of doing so, and yet here I am, like some science/fiction writer, reconstructing things out of imaginations' whole cloth.

Well, let's see. If I've got my facts straight the term *third world* did not come into usage until this century, when the European powers packed their bags and went home from Africa. Then all these new little nations appeared on the map and became collectively known as the Third World. Almost immediately it grew to include all nations anywhere which are unable to support themselves prosperously and pretty much lack the technology with which to try. First we had the New World and then by implication the Old World. Then we had the Free World and the Western World. I don't think we ever had a first world until suddenly we found ourselves with a third. Maybe we prosperous nations make up the second and the properly called First World is the Kingdom of God or something. Who knows? One does not hear the term *first world* bandied about very much.

Still it seems to me there should be a second world and, therefore, if we are not to be homeless, all prospering people must live in the first. I say there should be such a world, a midway world populated by nations that have gained ground in their efforts to leave the Third World yet still fall short of the gates to the first, because of such nations as China and Mexico and Brazil, to mention a few.

But if progress out of the Third World, through the Second to the First is possible, how about the reverse? Regress, for whatever reasons, from First World status to that of Second or even Third. Yes. Isn't Russia presently an example? And, while I hate to say it, I'm very much afraid that this nation is slipping toward the Second World itself. We're not there yet but we seem to be hopelessly in debt and we keep losing manufacturing at an alarming rate to other nations that can produce goods cheaper. We rebuilt both Germany and Japan after World War Two, an unheard of thing, and now they outshine us. Both countries export more to us than we can make and sell to them.

And then there's the immigration picture. That's changed drastically since World War Two. Now there come to our shores and borders, both legally and illegally, droves and droves of poor Asians, Blacks and Hispanics, no longer seeking new and better lives for themselves but life itself, many dying before they can ever get here. They swamp our schools with their young and smother our hospital emergency rooms and swell our welfare roles way past the breaking point. We have enough under-privileged poor—women who make a living producing babies; men who scoff at minimum wage and live better on welfare. Who needs this added influx of poor and uneducated people from all over the world? Fortunately, the Asians, mostly, are proud. Or, at any rate, they appear to have their own kind of work ethic. What's more, they push their kids to achieve in school here. But they still have too many of them. While the Blacks and the Hispanics . . . well, not only do they seem to indulge themselves irresponsibly in practically everything but they apparently consider themselves beaten in the race for a piece of the American pie before the race ever starts. Their kids drop out of school and then as adults they won't work either. While the schools, with so many of them to deal with, become constantly less able to properly prepare anybody to succeed anywhere in America. We're slipping all the time. This current so-called X-generation is the first in our history that cannot expect to have a better life than their parents had.

Moreover, our government caters to these people. Oh, it postures about stanching the flow. But the handouts and the programs, you don't see them disappearing. If anything, they increase. These people vote, of course. The legal new immigrants as soon as they can become citizens. Their 18 year old offspring are automatically citizens. 18 year olds born in this country, even if their illegal parents can never hope to gain citizenship, can vote. They can be martialed to vote to continue the hand-outs and the welfare programs. There are so many of them who can be so easily organized that they often outvote us, the privileged, affluent, professional, property-owning and educated population of the country, which typically limits itself to families of four. We had pretty much complete control of this country until the presidency of Andrew Jackson. Now, however, our hands tied and helpless, we feel forced to stand by and watch it go down the tubes. We feel so disenfranchised by PAC's and lobby groups and minority rights and special interest groups, by the sheer power of money itself to buy our politicians who supposedly represent all of us, not just those with the money to spare, by the encroaching power of government—the EPA, the IRS, the Department of everything—while what we want, most of us, is less and less government. Obviously, it was a much smaller country then, in the time of Andrew Jackson. And a whole lot less complicated. It lacked both Hawaii and Alaska. But the population was so much smaller, too. Today we who make up the PAPP & E population of the country are dwindling in numbers, while the new immigrant population and the welfare-loving, substance-addicted hordes who've taken over our cities and plague our streets with adolescent gangs continue to breed like rabbits with about as much thought to the consequences. We throw up our bound hands and say, hell, what's the use? Even the cops are overwhelmed. The country's going to the dogs and they're more of the goddamn dogs every day.

Well, my friends, we who wonder where is the invisible Second World, if we don't find a way to do something to stem the tide in this country, and I only wish I knew a way myself, we shall not only see the Second World, we shall have the chance to try our hand at leadership there. But the Second World is a transient world. Nations arrive there, hoping to stay no longer than they must. Nations like China and Mexico and Brazil seem plainly headed for the first. What shall we be doing? Continuing our uncontrollable slide until we find ourselves the most powerful nation in the third?

THE CONSTITUTION:

THEN & NOW

Now I think of myself as being as good an American as you can find these days. And a liberty-loving transplanted Texan as well. From Virginia I came, as did Sam Houston before me, and from a number of places between. I've read the Constitution of the United States. And I think it's the grandest, boldest, most generous constitution in the world. But I have to ask myself: how would it read if the same men had written it for today's population, not what they had in their small brave country two hundred odd years ago?

You know, for one thing, there was no welfare. That tiny population either worked or stole or it didn't eat. Sure, there must have been crime. But in many cases you had thieves driven by sheer physical necessity. It didn't take a battery of shrinks to figure out what motivated the crooks in those days. It was hunger or conscienceless greed.

And the only drug available generally was alcohol. Things were simpler in a lot of ways.

One thing a crook could count on, moreover, regardless of his motivation—there'd be no weights for him to lift nor TV in his cell. The gallows were far too cheap and practical. And, as for early release, he could forget about it.

And everybody owned a gun of course. Where the population was thinnest there were Indians. And, of course, anywhere wild game was a regular part of the public diet. And dueling as a means of settling one's differences was not illegal at that time. Possibly the founding fathers, when they got around to amending their immortal document, proposed the Second Amendment because it would have been such an impossible job to confiscate all the guns, had they ever wished to. But I'm beginning to get ahead of myself.

The point is the population for whom the founding fathers most immediately wrote their document was very different from what they would find today. They tried to look ahead, to be sure. We all know that. But, wise as they were, they could not have foreseen our country as it has become: polarized, for instance, which seems to be a negative result of immigration unfortunately. Did we open our gates too wide or did we fail to insist that all who come here become Americans and cease to be whatever they were when they arrived?

Which question having asked, I hasten to add that I don't mean we should abolish St. Patrick's Day. Or Halloween. These are picturesque and folksy things. Deeply rooted in myth and legend. Archetypical stuff, if you like, should you happen to be a Jungian. But the 16th of September or the 5th of May are both celebrations of Mexican independence. It's not right, it is in fact divisive, for some people living in this country to demand equal time for their abandoned political/historical holidays simply because the rest of us celebrate the 4th of July. I could go on and not even have to mention Chinese New Year or June 'Teenth. There's enough polarization to point to by the fact that Houston now has Chinese street signs, that too many of our teenagers of all ethnic origin feel the need to be in violent and destructive gangs, that our blacks, too many of them, look upon "whitey", A. K. A., "the man" as still their implacable enemy and that everybody seems to have their hand out to the government to make their lives right, instead of simply working to make things better themselves. Work does not have to mean just jobs and wages, you know.

Because of the erosion of our once sharply defined attitudes toward work, coupled with an increasingly popular idea that somebody owes us a living; because of our loss due to polarization of a binding sense of national unity, until the noisiest "patriots" among us have become a polarized fringe group themselves; because of drugs; because of growing cynicism and disillusionment; because of an over-liberalized policy toward criminals, coupled with a slow-down in the administration of whatever justice there is; because of a growing disparity between the rich and the poor, coupled with a shrinking of the former population while the latter have multiplied like rabbits; because of all these things and more our country has become a different place than that in which the founding fathers lived and breathed and had their being. In which they thought and put to paper their best ideas, committing to the task their fondest hopes for all Americans to follow them, indeed mankind.

They were white, mostly Anglo-Saxon and principally Protestant. Today they would find themselves in an ethnic group, one of many that make up this dramatically different country.

In those days the puny country of thirteen colonies mustered an army willing to take on the British Empire. Not every colonist wanted anything to do with it and those who did suffered a great deal. But they brought the British Army to its knees. One of my ancestors was a Tory but another served as a sergeant in the Continental Army. Now we have an army supposed to be the best and best equipped in the world and all it can do effectively is to beat up on third world thugs. We've come a long way down the hill of decline just since World War Two it seems.

Another thing about colonial times was the sheer cost of getting here. Not everybody was willing to pay it. Not just the money for the fare but the considerable ardors of an ocean voyage in those days. And nothing but work when you landed. Today's welfare dependents and dope addicts would never have considered it.

Naturally there were rich young entrepreneurs who came here too, notably those who established the tobacco and cotton plantations in the southern colonies. Also there were men with the wherewithal to build or buy ships, who came to make still more money trading. That's what the colonies did to support and enrich themselves: produce and ship raw materials to Europe. All the cities that grew and prospered in early America were trading centers. Washington alone, which became the capital after Philadelphia, had no part in trade; and it remained an anachronistic and pretentious looking small town with muddy streets until well into the 19th century.

The people who came here came for the opportunities. The opportunity to make a buck, obviously, and not always an honest one, but also the opportunity to practice freely whatever their religion was, and there were many unpopular in Europe at the time. However, there were enough educated men of philosophical bent who came here in pursuit of more than wealth or religious freedom, a dream. A dream of a land in which there could be both prosperity and liberty.

From the birth of the Renaissance in western Europe, from somewhere around the middle to the end of the 15th century, educated men in England and France had entertained such ideas. But they were radical still and called for a new place if they were to be realized. To this land and in that hope, therefore, came the fathers of the founding fathers of our country.

I suppose I cannot close this little exercise in historical speculation without first saying something about God and family. The words "In God we trust" still appear on our coins and there's the popular expression, "as American as family and Mom's apple pie". I don't think there were any atheists among the founding fathers, Jefferson and Franklin being about as close to that extreme as anybody came in that crowd. Of course, a lot of them were religious for purely practical reasons, as opposed to being passionately devout. Yet God enjoyed a preeminence in those days that He can lay little claim to today.

Why? There are many reasons. The advance of knowledge for one. Man has learned more about this world and the universe in the last two hundred years than anybody guessed in the previous ten thousand. In the last hundred years a lot of people have come to believe that science will eventually explain everything. I'm not so sure I may not one day be one of them. But something will always be theory. Like a theoretical definition of God that's consistent with all the scientific facts available. Creation becomes the cosmic egg at the bottom of a collapsed black hole. But the black hole turns white in another context. And around we go again. Or somebody does. There is no stasis. The only thing eternal is change.

Then there's the erosion of ideals generally, due to growing cynicism, disillusionment and doubt already mentioned. This has had its effect on the family. But the main things I think that have undermined traditional family solidarity are the growth of communication and knowledge and the fact that we move around so much. Now from generation to generation the world changes incredibly, while moving around, thanks to modern transportation, has become easy. New York to San Francisco in the same day. Compare this to a time when the California coast might as well have been Mars, if people knew it was even there.

Families lose their solidarity and disintegrate when they become too splintered and separated. The isolated son in Seattle who has left the nest in Miami learns to do the things for himself that his mother used to do. And the things he did with his dad, he learns to do with others or without. What is left is the generation gap. They don't understand each other anyway. So his calls become less frequent and at last he may even cease to write. That is if the schools have taught him to write, because almost his entire education may be television, CD disks and videos.

Two hundred years ago education was pretty formalized and rigid. Children learned what their fathers had been taught. The world was changing at a slower pace and there was continuity from generation to generation as a result. My father was born in

1896. I was born in 1930. In no more than the thirty-four years before my father had a son, man leapt from the saddle of a horse to the seat of an automobile to the cockpit of an airplane. And in the next thirty-two years before I had a son, man leapt almost to the moon! When my father was born the Bell telephone had been patented for twenty years. By the time my first son was born television was in all but the poorest homes in America and some few had color TV.

Change is constant, unavoidable, irreconcilable. Once you're caught in its sweep there's no going back. And we, all of us, have seen more change in the last half century than mankind saw in the half millennium before that.

Much of this change has been good. That is, it's apparent how our lives have been made better by it. But much of it has had the effect of being disturbing, destabilizing, even threatening.

As individuals we are as much the product of our environments as of our genes. When the environment is sure and stable so is its product. I submit that the environment two hundred years ago, despite the Indians, fatal accidents, war, pestilence and fevers for which the doctors had no cure, was essentially stable. Indians and disease could be depended upon. People did not expect life to be without pain and mortal danger and they tended to accept these with the same unthinking fatalism as their fellow animals. That too has changed.

We have come to think that life need not be insecure. That the government, the medical profession, anybody with enough manpower and equipment should make the world safe for us. But the "indians" today are unpredictable. They are crazy on drugs or they're pathologically ruthless to a degree that seems unparalleled in human history. And then we have cancer and AIDS. If either existed two hundred years ago they were unidentified.

The point is that the world has become uncertain again and we are no longer disposed to accept that. And a crazy world can produce a lot of crazy people. The U. S. population in 1790 was less than four million. Today it's more than two hundred and fifty million. If a mere one percent of the population in 1790 refused to live by the rules, for whatever reason, we're only talking about forty thousand people, less than that, actually, that the law could find itself having to deal with. The same percentage of two hundred and fifty million, though, is a whopping two and a half million! Which is a lot of non-conformists, deviants, anarchists, crazies and bad guys to be reckoned with. As the population grows so does the number of malcontents. As for AIDS, the same could be said of homosexuals and promiscuous heterosexuals. Cancer I think we'll find eventually is an indirect consequence of both pollution and life style. Two hundred years ago the greatest source of pollution in the cities was probably horse manure, or inadequate sewerage generally, more or less natural pollution, while the life styles, either urban or rural, were spartan by comparison with those of today.

Uncertainty and sudden unpredictable and deadly threats— that's the stuff of today's world.

Which was true two centuries ago also. But today's "Indians" are drug-crazed addicts turned criminal, violent teenagers in gangs, paranoid political anarchists. Even if the percentage of lawless in the population has remained the same, which I doubt, two and a half million is a lot of crazies on the loose. Personally I think the changes in the socio/economic environment during the last twenty decades have produced more.

When we were willing to take our own chances the bad things in the environment had less effect on us. Oh, they made us careful but they didn't warp our minds. Today we expect the government, the army, the police, the doctors, anybody but ourselves to protect us from all ill. We've surrendered that mind-saving dose of fatalism to higher authority. Today the ills of the world beset us as they always have, only now, since we've enabled them, they also twist our minds.

In other words, not only are there now something like sixty-three times more of us than there were in 1787, sixty-three or more for every single misfit alive at that time, but we have also let ourselves become vulnerable in ways that people then were not. We want the burdens of dealing with a complex, apparently hostile world lifted from us. Let the government do it. We want protection. We don't see why we should suffer at all. If the government, if the doctors, if the police all did their jobs right, then we should not have to suffer we say. The writers of a constitution for the people of this nation today would have to be aware of this.

We completely overlook the possibility that the world may seem so hostile because, worldwide, there are just too many of us. We are stretching the planet to its limits. Economically, the wealth simply isn't enough to distribute itself so far. Already writers and philosophers envisage the Earth of the future, it's continents paved over. Only where humans could not possibly live does the land look like it does now. The ice-clad rock faces of the Himalayas, for example.

A constitution written for us today could not possibly grant us the freedoms we presently enjoy. We are too many, too polarized, too apathetic, too vulnerable, too unwilling to accept the responsibility for our own actions. It would seem that we neither deserve such freedoms nor should we be trusted with them.

It is a shame, a crying shame for us and mankind, a terrible historical tragedy in the making. This is the only nation in the history of the world to have undertaken so grand a dream. I only hope, I don't know how, I pray therefore that its dissolution is still avoidable.

Awake America! From your separate and irreconcilable dreams of pre-cradle to grave dependence upon anything but yourselves. Find ways to unite and become Americans. Let us become a nation of one language as a starting point. Gather the threads of your unraveling families and knit them back together. Quit being so utterly helpless and take charge of your own lives. Be willing to suffer the consequences of failure and try, try again. The enemy is always out there, bent on your destruction. But take heart! You are at least his equal, if you are determined and strong. Indeed God may find ways to help those who help themselves. But the rest I don't think He bothers with at all.

THE SECOND

AMENDMENT

The Second Amendment to the Constitution of the United States of America states that: "A well regulated militia, being necessary to the security of a free State, the right of the people to keep and bear Arms, shall not be infringed." Or, as Webster puts it, in the ninth edition of the New Collegiate Dictionary: shall not be "encroach[ed] upon in a way that violates law or the rights of another." Now that seems pretty clear. So what is all the argument about? The lawmakers of this country are surely listening to something. Confusion, I think. But let's see what we can make of it ourselves.

Now I'm no lawyer and, to tell the truth, based on my experiences with them, I dislike and distrust the breed. With the exception of my father, who was the last lawyer I knew to be motivated by anything like integrity. But I can read and I do have some understanding of our language. Moreover, I am a gun lover. And, midst all the hue and cry being raised these days, it seems incumbent upon all of us gun lovers, whether shooters, hunters, collectors or all three, to take a position on gun control and defend it. Okay. Ready on the firing line! Here goes.

The amendment does not actually give anybody the right to keep and bear arms. Not the way I read it. Rather it assumes that the right already exists. Nor does it unilaterally guarantee the right either. For there's a qualifier. It says that since a free State needs a militia for its own security—but a "well regulated militia", you'll note, which gives the federal government some inroads right there—"the right of the people to keep and bear arms shall not be infringed". In other words, you have the right, because you always had it and it cannot be encroached upon, but you have a responsibility that goes along with it, once you become a citizen of a free and constitutional new nation.

I think the government, acting on the wording of the second amendment, should be saying this. But the government is so screwed up now, who knows what it's trying to say. Nevertheless, what it should be saying to us with respect to our guns is: Yes, of course, you can have them. But up to a point. There are limitations. True, we can't rescind or nullify your right to them, because we need people ready and able to defend the country (and the Ninth Amendment makes it difficult, too), but we can damn sure regulate them and don't you forget it. Our need is for a militia but there can be no militia without regulations. And so will ours be. You can have your guns, provided they are not inconsistent with the needs of an effective military organization and provided that what you do with them serves the purposes of such an organization. And one more thing—provided you stand ready to defend your country, or the public good, by serving in such a militia, should that ever be necessary.

You can practice shooting, therefore, where the object is to improve your marksmanship or to increase your overall competency with your weapon or weapons. You can hunt also, because, presumably, hunting will increase your ability to move stealthily in the field. But you cannot just raise hell or run around shooting with no defined purpose. Okay? Or engage in criminal acts. Such things cannot be tolerated.

You can collect guns of past wars and eras but we might see fit to put a limitation on how many guns of new manufacture you should own (no more than _____, say, for every distinct type of shooting you engage in), because more than a certain number of new guns seems to be excessive for a potential militiaman. How many assault rifles do you need to be practiced and proficient with one, I'm tempted to ask? However, I personally think it's a mistake to outlaw assault rifles *per se*. I think it's unconstitutional, actually.

Since we look to you to serve us with your arms, your government might go on to ask, what arms of appropriate types you own and with which you are most proficient? If we should ever need you to defend us, wouldn't we want to use you to your best capability? We feel not embarrassed, therefore, to suggest that you might demonstrate your readiness to serve your country. We might ask you to attend meetings once a month, as National Guardsmen or Reservists do, or join a sanctioned club, or complete courses in firearms related subjects; and if you do not, we might say in that case, "Well, sorry—having failed to demonstrate a readiness to serve the needs of a well regulated national militia, your right to keep and bear arms of current manufacture has been indefinitely suspended." Something like the Swiss do. Citizen soldiers. Sure you have a right to have a gun. But there are no rights without responsibilities. Are there?

So what if you're a conscientious objector? You can't stand ready to bear arms against anybody, invaders of your country notwithstanding. If you're a citizen of the United States I'd say you were in trouble as a gun owner. You have no business with a gun in the first place. Regardless of its peaceful uses, a gun is first and foremost a weapon. If you cannot use one to defend yourself or your country, don't have one. It's so simple as to seem obvious.

So what else seems simple or obvious? Are there any kinds of conclusions we can draw at this point? Can we state a position here? My position is that the government, misguided by a bunch of vociferous alarmists, is going at this thing all wrong. Instead of proceeding to outlaw guns, what they ought to be doing is outlawing irresponsible and inappropriate gun users. I'm as alarmed by the rampant violence in this country as is anybody.

And I agree that something must be done. But guns alone aren't responsible. Somebody always pulls their triggers. Go after those guys. One possible way to do so has been outlined. Regulate the ownership of guns, not by prohibitive taxation and licensing, but in more constructive ways that underline the responsibility one assumes by owning a gun. Weed out the people who can't or won't accept that responsibility. Don't take all their guns away from them. For that's not constitutional. But deny them any legal use of the firearms they refuse to consider a responsibility as well as property. Don't go after the people who pose no threat to anybody but the enemies of these United States of America.

The Nazis used the technique of making the innocent pay for the crimes of the guilty. That is, they shot a number of innocent people for every single German killed by the resistance. Our government appears to be trying something similar, apparently moving to deprive lawful and responsible gun owners of their arms, in the hopes of discouraging criminals from running the added risks, or paying the higher prices, that obtaining arms for themselves might then entail. It's wrong headed and, what's more, it's unconstitutional!

THE TEXAS HILL

COUNTRY

In THE GREEN HILLS OF AFRICA Hemingway is forever entering some new country. And he doesn't mean crossing political boundaries either. For Hemingway any area that has a certain topographical homogeneity, where only certain trees and shrubs and flowers grow, is a country, irrespective of invisible political lines that may cross it. Just so is the Texas Hill Country, an area of central Texas, south of Dallas and west of the Colorado River, just west of Austin but north of San Antonio and Uvalde and bordered on the west by the higher ground of the Edwards Plateau. This country is characterized by cropped limestone hills covered with a thin layer of topsoil. But not so well that the rock fails to show through. It's everywhere. The rainfall is not great. Winters and summers can be very dry. Waterless creek beds, down which tumble sun-bleached rocks and boulders abound. There are, however, some year round rivers, principally the LLano and the lovely Guadalupe that flows through Kerrville, San Marcos and New Braunfels. Everyone in Texas has heard of tubing on the Guadalupe.

Except for its headwaters up on the Edwards the Guadalupe flows with this magical bluish green. It almost makes you swear the water must be dyed. The Llano does that, too, where it's deep enough, but this is only for a part of its course. Near Junction the Llano runs green but it's a lighter, less enchanted color.

The Hill Country is a hunter's paradise. Deer and turkey are ubiquitous, while half the former cattle ranches seem to operate as pay-as-you-shoot hunting preserves, boasting bison, elk and kudu, as well as an assortment of smaller Asian and African species. The country offers a near ideal year around climate for us humans, too. In fact it is the main summer camp area in Texas, as well as a winter refuge for countless out-of-state seniors who own RV's. But the endlessly fascinating thing about the Hill Country to me is the enormous variety of life it supports, *flora* and *fauna*, with only that thin layer of topsoil to work with, most of it mixed with shattered rock as it is. There are pastures in this country that grow more rock than they do grass.

Once this area was Comanche and Apache hunting territory. I've read accounts by soldiers stationed at forts out here in those days of turkeys roosting by the thousands within hailing distance of their outposts. White men of course ran off all the Indians and carved the country up into cattle ranches. There was also a lot of cypress in the creek and river bottoms that ran fuller in those days. The cypress was all cut, too. Precious few old trees remain today. Cypress won't rot, you know, so it makes superb siding and shingles. While the cattle over grazed the land and killed the grass and so the topsoil blew away.

The next invaders were the cedars, or junipers, actually. They can take root in sheer rock and, once established, will kill everything but themselves. They grow faster than the oaks and other trees and can cut them off from the sun. And they take so much water from the land that nothing can grow under them. Perhaps the coating of dead needles they put on the ground contributes to this dead space beneath them. But I've been told of places that had surface springs until the cedars overran them. When the cedars were all cut off the springs reappeared.

It is the roots of grass and bushes and trees that hold the precious topsoil against the gully-washer rains that visit our country in spring and fall. Especially the shallow rooted grasses. But all roots must spread out over the limestone here. They cannot go down. You have only to try to dig a hole in this country to appreciate this reality. Likewise, any plant that wants some acidity or iron in the soil, like an azalea, for instance, will not grow here, let alone the difficulty of making a hole deep enough to plant it in. But, my God, the variety of vegetation that, during the spring, does flourish here! And hangs grimly on during the rest of the year. The wild flowers alone are just incredible. Many of these, like the bluebonnets, simply dry up and blow away. But they leave their very durable seeds.

It is late spring as I write. This time of year Houston, which I left to come here, is green also. But all the same green, grass and trees alike. Here, as I look out my window, I see spread between the pale yellows of grasses beginning to dry, and the browns of dead leaves, and the near black of the shadows and twisted tree trunks, almost every shade of green imaginable. An artist could sit here where I am and have a field day mixing blues and yellows, white, red and black. While above the broken canopy of leaves there's a Wedgwood blue sky across which drift puffy white clouds.

My place of eleven acres is blessed to have little cedar. Still the EPA in its wisdom, in its heroic effort to save some warbler from extinction, would not have me cut what there is. The warbler uses strips of cedar bark to build its nest. Well, the warbler wasn't threatened with extinction by the Comanches. And in those days, as I understand, there was a whole hell of lot less cedar than now. My land looks like everywhere this country might have looked then—grass and stunted oak forests. None of these oaks grow very tall. However, the post oaks and the Spanish oaks have perhaps the greatest capability.

But there are also sumac, hackberry, wild cherry and redbud. I have not seen so much naturally seeded redbud growing anywhere as I have on my little place here. And in the open patches, where there is constant sun, there's *nopal*, or prickly pear cactus. While, in secluded spots that see more shade, wild fox grape vines entwine the tree limbs. And at night, sometimes following only the glowing path of the Milky Way across the sky, deer wander as if they owned my place.

How would I describe this country, if you don't already have a picture of it? I think I'd have to repeat that it's choppy, billowing like a wind driven sea, as one gazes over it, the exposed rock giving the appearance of myriad whitecaps. And where the highway cuts through it, as does the Interstate 10 on its way from Beaumont to El Paso, one can count its layers, sometimes crushed rock and clay but oftentimes solid limestone, in which the drill holes for the dynamite still show.

This country looks old, as if it's been here, surviving, in spite of the stinginess of the elements, for all time at least. Some of the cuts that the rivers have made are more than a hundred feet deep. I don't think I've ever seen such old and yet vibrant looking country. The Appalachians come to mind but one knows they must be younger. All this country was once ancient sea bed, they tell me.

It gives me the idea that it's a good place to grow old in. There's such a cranky determination to survive about it, despite all the rock and the suffocating cedars. It celebrates life in such a variety of, if stunted ways, I may do well to emulate it.

ON THE EDGE OF THE

EDWARDS

The Hill Country or the Edwards Plateau, as some like to call it—although one look at a topographical map will show you that the Edwards is an area above 2000 feet, a delta-like configuration where the High Plains flowing deep over the Panhandle spill out into the great heart of Texas, while the country leading up to this from the directions of San Antonio and Austin is the Hill country—in particular then the irregular rim country that fits the extended fingers of the Edwards like a glove might fit a distorted hand, is an extra-ordinary and quite enchanting region.

Rocky hills cut by rock-walled, rock-filled streams, many of which flow with water only when it rains, and rain is likely in the form of a cloudburst and very localized. Dwarfed trees because almost all the rain comes down in this manner. Flash floods are not uncommon. Nor is hail, which is a reason many of the houses have tin rather than composition shingle roofs.

Game abounds in the form of deer and turkey. And now of course exotics too: axis and fallow deer, elk, bison and many other species of imported hoofed creatures. And there's a far greater variety of shrubs and trees than I would have believed on first seeing this country. In the spring and into summer wild flowers color the country side. First the bluebonnets and the Indian paintbrushes, followed by the wild sage and all the yellow flowers along roadsides and in the fields. The country is greenest in spring, to be sure, but fascinating at any time of the year. In spring there are a hundred hues and shades of green, but as the grasses dry in summer only the trees and shrubs retain their color. In the fall, when many trees lose their leaves, the live oak and the juniper do not; and one is treated not only to their deep greens against the blanket of brown and yellowing grasses but to the bright yellow of the sumacs and red of the Spanish oaks as well. And winter is the time of the year to hunt.

Throughout the year the humidity remains low. While summers can be hot they're nothing like the misery of the coastal plain. I lived in Houston before I bought my place near Kerrville and, for my part, you could rename Houston, Bombay. Perhaps that's why so many southeast Asian people seem to like it there.

The longest finger of the Edwards extends east just north of Fredericksburg. There's a loop one can make through that area called the Willow City Loop. In spring, when so many wild flowers are in bloom, this makes a great little trip. It only takes about an hour, unless you stop a lot to admire the flowers or the views. So take your picnic lunch and make a day of it. About 12 miles northeast of Fredericksburg on Texas Highway 16 you'll come upon the paved road to Willow City. Turn right. If you go a little further and arrive in Eckert you can also turn right there. In either case the Willow City Loop will carry you back to Highway 16, which you can use to return to Fredericksburg or Kerrville.

Kerrville makes a convenient base from which to explore and enjoy this border country.

The next longest finger of the Edwards extends southeast just north of the little city surrounded by hills through which flows the Guadalupe River. Kerrville has some very comfortable and attractive motels. Some less picturesque but very economical ones too. And some entirely satisfactory restaurants. Two I could recommend are Joe's Jefferson Street Cafe and Kathy's On the River.

Another trip you might want to consider starts in Kerrville and can be made to include the YO Ranch. The YO offers a late morning, lunch included, tour of its exotic game farm operation. You get to feed some of the tamer animals, the eland, for example. But watch out for the ostrich. And then you sit down to an all-you-can-eat, absolutely delicious lunch before it's all over.

Anyway, what you do is follow Kerrville's Junction Highway west to Ingram, where you bear left on Texas Highway 39. Which follows the Guadalupe River to Hunt. There you want to look for FM 1340 on your right. If you go too far, stop at The Store, also on your right, to ask directions. FM 1340 follows the north fork of the river almost to its source. If you turn left when the road dumps into Texas Highway 41 you'll reach the front gate of the YO Ranch in about a mile. You can use Highway 41 in the opposite direction to Mountain Home to connect with Texas Highway 27 to get back to Ingram and Kerrville.

This is a very scenic trip, offering views of the Guadalupe, shaded by giant cypress trees, as well as glimpses of the many fine homes and summer camps that line it between Ingram and Hunt. FM 1340 is a meandering climbing road that gets you up on the Edwards Plateau. And passes the Kerr Wildlife Management area. While the ride back into Ingram on Highway 27 takes you past the Texas Parks and Wildlife Department fish hatchery, where I've heard they're developing a strain of largemouth bass with a tendency to almost hook themselves. 27 also boasts some really great overlooks of Johnson Creek valley. The tour offered by the YO is by reservation only. So call ahead. The tab when I did it a couple of years ago was $24.00 a head.

Assuming now that you're staying in Kerrville you still owe it to yourself to spend at least a part of a day in Fredericksburg. One way to get there from Kerrville, so that you arrive about lunchtime, is to take FM 783, the Harper Road, across the Junction Highway from the Inn of the Hills, where you might be staying, actually. From Harper take FM 2093 to Fredericksburg. This little road follows the Pedernales River more or less and wanders through some pretty ranching country. Goats, lots of goats, and some sheep and cattle. In Fredericksburg be sure to enjoy a German lunch and then go shopping with everyone else on the Hautstrasse or Main Street. Or visit the Chester Nimitz museum. If you miss 2093, stop at Dauna's on the corner. They'll get you back on track.

If you really want an appreciation of the change in elevation that divides the Hill Country from the Edwards Plateau, go to Junction. To get there from Kerrville take Interstate 10 west. On a topographical map the cut the Llano River makes flowing out of the Edwards Plateau looks like the Grand Canyon. Or the cleft between the thumb and fingers of the distorted ape's hand that the Edwards Plateau somewhat resembles. On the ground it's less dramatic but still impressive. Unfortunately, there's not a great deal else to see in Junction. Unless it's Easter. They do an annual outdoor passion play at that time that draws a lot of people.

The last long excursion you might make in this rock-studded, stunted country, where so much life depends on so little topsoil, originates again in Harper, on the side of the longest finger of the monkey's hand. Go west out of Harper on U.S. Highway 290 to the junction of FM 385. Take this north up over the finger and down into the lower country drained by the James and the Llano rivers to London, a quaint little town that seems lifeless but which harbors a dance hall known throughout this whole part of Texas. From London take U.S. Highway 377 to Mason and then U.S. Highway 87 to Brady. The views are panoramic of escarpments and the rolling country side is enlivened by exposed red earth and rock. There's a dam and a reservoir at Brady where they say the croppie fishing can be lively. On your way back take the pictures you failed to take in the morning.

Finally, one little trip before you leave Kerrville should be to the Cowboy Artists of America Museum, reached by crossing the river on Highway 16 South and then taking a left on Texas Highway 173. Nor should you go home without sampling a burger or the barbecue at the Lone Oak Store on FM 479, Exit 492 off the I-

10. But you can get there a very pretty way by following Highway 27 out of Ingram until it junctures with FM 479 just past the bridge over Dry Branch Creek. Don't hit any of the sheep. They wander all over this road as it follows Dry Branch Creek to its apparent source, somewhere underground. Before then, however, you will have spied the Lone Oak Store. Enjoy your lunch.

TO MY SONS: A LETTER AFTER THE FASHION OF LORD CHESTERFIELD IMPARTING SOME WISDOM OF THEIR GRANDFATHER

Sons, the two most important principles by which a man should guide his life are honor and discipline. A man without honor is a man without hope of Heaven, as your grandfather would have said, but a man without discipline cannot be an honorable one. The world is full enough with weak men who have the best of intentions, as well as scoundrels who cannot see past each moment's mean desire. Of course, I do not hope for you that at my age you should find yourself in either group. Not that you will either—in fact, I am sure you won't—but allow me to discuss with you in this manner the means by which you can avoid such a fate surely.

I'm not sure you fully understand the concept of personal honor. I'm sure you know all the catch phrases, such as, "A man's word is his bond" or ". . . to thine ownself be true . . .", etc., etc. but there's more to it than just refusing to tell a lie, either to yourself or to someone else.

A man of honor is a man who can be depended upon. He will always behave in a certain way. He will live by the Golden Rule or, at any rate, he will try to. And just as he will shrink from knowingly telling a lie, he won't suffer being lied to. Except to forgive an act of weakness or ignorance in another, however. Moreover, he is loathe to promise something and then fail to deliver it. Similarly he expects all promises made to him to be kept. But always he's aware that not all men are so strong or as fortunate as he himself may be, and, thus, that which he could never abide in himself he stands ready to forgive in others. Furthermore, as he himself is truthful, and most importantly to himself, he wants only the truth to be said of him. He wants nothing that is not justly his. He wants no wage he hasn't earned. He will abide no lie to be told of him, therefore, nor any exaggeration to be made. And he won't rest until any such lie or exaggeration has been undone. As he would defend his own good reputation, so is he ready to defend that of any other falsely accused or badly spoken of. Yet those who receive credit for laudable things he may have done he may modestly leave alone. Justice is most sacred to him but tempered with mercy and compassion. It is honor, son, that would keep us in God's way. It is the cultivation of honor and the preservation of if it that gives us the courage to die.

But, my son, I must remind you that without discipline one cannot be an honest man. Take an untrained child for example. It knows no restraint and yields to every temptation that comes its way. And so would we. We'd all be untrained children were it not for discipline.

The discipline of the law, of course, will deter many of us from being criminals. But the law does not equally persuade us to be honest. Honesty, that attribute of an honorable man, is a result of self-discipline, son, which is a system of behavior control that has no resources outside ourselves. We are its only legislators and its only officers of enforcement. There are no outside police to blow their whistles when we stray. Any whistle that blows must be the voice of our own conscience. Any arrests that are made must be acts of self-denial. It's incumbent upon each of us to find the good and the honorable way for ourselves, the only way after all if we are to become true gentlemen, for that term encompasses far more than a mere knowledge of polite ways and manners. Simple obedience of the laws will keep us from committing criminal acts but there is no such enforceable code that can coerce us onto the gentle track. Onto that we must guide ourselves. And it takes strength to stay there, too.

The law is a response to evil, you see, and thank God we had the wisdom to devise it. Honor and the establishment of one's personal code of honor are responses of the soul within us, of our love of God and of our longing to see His ways prevail. The law is essentially negative in that it is prohibitive. Honor, however, is a positive element in our lives. In those countries where there can be said to be a rule of law the law is determined by the will of a majority of the people who must live under it, but one's code of honor must be forged by one for himself. Beaten out of the raw metals of what the world calls its wisdom. Or smelted and alloyed by the divine breath of God's help. A code of honor is a thing we must each devise and impose upon ourselves. And without self-discipline this will simply not be possible.

POEMS

TEARS FOR A SPARROW

There was a time when even sparrows died for cause.
A child could shed a tear and learn of death.
A little tear, of course, a little lesson
But hardly wasted just for being small.

There was a time when, if you were perceptive,
If, more than that, you cared,
There was truth in little places
And its value lay in finding it,
For so many missed its shine.
And now you have to wonder
If all those tiny glimmerings
Were ever really there.

Perhaps they were winking rust spots
In the pitted hide of the maiden
In which God lies pierced and silent
And has for a long, long time.

Perhaps they were glinting nail points,
Thrust first through wood in building
But then through God for blundering
And getting in the way.

Perhaps they were glistening blood drops,
Flung from pulverized men lauding God,
Dancing wildly to echoing bomb crashes
Against which no tears can be heard.

We shed glycerin tears for mass murder.
Weeping Buddha has tears of pure jade.
But there's still worth in deaths of mere sparrows,
In distilled tears of grief from the small;
Yes, there is truth in tears for dead sparrows.
Else how's one to glimpse a bare soul?

Charlottesville, VA, 1958

ODE TO A TOAD

Believer without belief,
Seeker with no object.
Lover without love,
Journey with no destination.
Asker without any answers,
Revolutionary devoid of a cause.
Reactionary impelled toward the future,
Godless and seeking God.

Starving still in the bakery,
Lost on the road map itself.

Man alone befriended,
In whom people believe, but why?
Something, surely, but what—
Somebody, yes, but whom?

Wondering at stars and children,
The eyes of puppies and birds.
Entranced by the world and living,
But crushed by a single dead toad.

Modern man or ageless,
Son of God or damned?
Is this where history has brought us,
Or is Truth the corpse of a toad?

San Francisco, CA, 1960

WHERE LEGIONS BLAZE

I always thought of death so dark
That consciousness could not survive.
We do endure, though not alive,
In hearts of those we've left behind.
Yet now I'm not content with this;
I cannot bear to think her light
So snuffed that nowhere in the World it shines.

Our brains are like computers, don't they say—
Electrochemical transceivers, sending and responding to
Faint waves, whose ripples spread through Space and
Time,

Yet never reach the end,
If Einstein is to be believed.
Since we awoke and first perceived,
We've tweaked the strings of cosmic webs.

So do these webs thus heave the sighs
And billow with the dreams of Man?
Are *they* aware since *we* once were,
But more and more with muddled ken?
They bear the imprint now of all;
We *are* Mankind:
It *is* the total that survives.

Her light therefore shall always shine,
But as one flame where legions blaze,
And more and more arrive each day.
I keep her face in every room,
So when I die, as they should now,
My thoughts will join
To reinforce her tiny glow.

Houston, April, 1990

THE TASTE OF TRUTH

"Bite its neck," my uncle said.
The stricken bird fell out the air
And struck the ground and lay,
Not dead nor quick enough to run,
A tattered heap of trembling feathers
Anchored by the shot embedded in it by my gun.

"Bite its neck," my uncle said,
Who never missed and seldom crippled
When a covey rose.
There was with him and his unkempt old gun
A fluid oneness I envied much.
He hid it, though, 'neath old and sturdy hunting clothes.

"Bite its neck," my uncle said.
Were any things more comely made than game birds
are?
Or any time so handsome as the winter is?
Its duns and browns, the reds and yellows and the ever-
greens.
And what, I asked, the craft of man,
Is more artf'ly wrought than a fowling piece?

"Bite its neck," my uncle said.
I held it in my hand, a hen,
Her yellowed throat convulsing.
Could he be serious? I eyed my uncle,
Master hunter, and knew at once
That I would do just what he said.

"Bite its neck," my uncle said.
The salty blood flowed 'tween my teeth,
The doomed bird shook, I felt it die.
And in my mind the winter scene and pretty prey,
The grace, *finesse* of well-placed shots, all quivered too
And dissolved away, before the flood—my taste of truth.

Houston, fall, 1988

MARGARET ELIZABETH

The sweetness of my empty hours
I fill with thoughts of you.
I see your face, your morning face,
Unpainted, as your soul shines through.

The soul I touched at first
And woke it from its slumbering;
The soul I teased and breathed upon
And fanned it from its smoldering.

The soul I held at last, caressing it,
Until it moaned and cried.
The soul, like mine, caught in the storm
That we've unleashed and now must ride.

Ah, dear, to kiss again in quiet waters,
Where breezes sweet and calm collect.
Meteors don't all burn up, you know;
Some do enrich the earth where they impact.

Houston, 1993

BARB'RA JEAN AND
THE DIAMOND MAN.

Well, once there was a diamond man
To whom his baubles were but stock in trade.
And yet found he a girl who'd never seen such.
"I'm Barb'ra Jean," confessed the maid.

"Take one of these. I love thee much,"
Told Barb'ra Jean the diamond man.

"Oh, how it sparkles! How it shines!"
Said she, her heart a-flutter like a fan.
"No man has one ever done so much for me."
"Then give it back," proposed her diamond man.
"I'll put it in a ring for thee,
And give it thee this Valentine's.

No rose nor card nor other thing
Did she desire that lovers pray—
His ring alone, his promised ardor—
But came and went that lovers' day,
And he forgot, beset with labor,
So much demand did each day bring.

"So just where *is* it?" asked Barb'ra Jean,
"That which you swore to me this day?"
"What did I swear? I . . . I have been working.
I've had no time for thought or play.
So name the thing—whatever's yours—an end to shirking."
But look at him and sigh did Barb'ra Jean.

"Anything I do not want," made bold the maid to whisper.
"If I must name what you have named,
I want it less, believe me. I'll do without. I did before."
"Oh God, it was a ring," he blanched, "Indeed I must be blamed.
I've been so busy I forgot. And me with dozens in my store."
"Forget again," said Barb'ra Jean, "and pray that you may prosper."

"Ah, prosper, hell!", he thought, "Indeed, I may have perished.
No blood is lost but love!" For once to one you cleave,

And think yourself clove unto, the heart shifts place
And in the chest cannot be found but rather on the sleeve.
And trifling things that once you bore, with seeming grace,
Can seem like darts, with poisoned tips, if coming from your
cherished.

Kerrville,February,1996

POEMS MY FATHER

WROTE

I had some problems relating to my father. In a novel I tried to present him as he really was, even quoting letters word for word and following the chronology of his life in scrupulous detail. To what purpose, you may ask? Did I hope somehow to expiate my own guilt? For guilt is what any decent son will feel when he thinks he does not love his father enough. Or that he fails to live up to his father's hopes. Or both, for that matter. I don't know. Perhaps. But of this much I'm sure. Some of my father still lives in me. I would not be whatever I am, trying to live whatever my life has become, had he not lived before me. And any man who tries to do anything, which he believes in his heart to be good, deserves at least our passing nod for his effort.

My father thought of himself as a sort of poet. The same notion has passed through my mind. You've seen some of my best efforts. Here now are some of his:

REBELLION

So full is life of punishments,
And debts and mortgages and rents,

And retributions for one's sins,
And pains from barking of one's shins,
And contrite feelings of remorse,
And nasty spills from a horrid horse,
And lonely loves and blighted hopes,
And many gummy misanthropes,
That frequently my soul rebels
And longs for the peace of infidels,
Who go their way so free and merry
With recompense unnecessary.
I long to burst the bonds that bind
My soul to being sweet and kind;
I long sometimes to be quite rude
And even on occasions crude;
I long to be indelicate
And nevermore a celibate;
I long to say just what I think
And take what I like to eat and drink;
But no, alas, I dream in vain—
The moving finger makes it plain
That life is fashioned in a mold
Which I can't crack till I'm too old.

A LOG AT SEA

It was only a useless floating log,
And nothing was at stake;
It lay beyond the breaking waves
An wallowed in their wake.

And yet it held my raptured gaze—
The struggle seemed so queer;
I wondered would it reach the shore
Or finally disappear.

Each shoreward wave would lift it high
And hurl it at the beach;
But with an odd dexterity
The log escaped its reach.

I watched it for an hour or more—
This fight for mastery—
The log's inanimate guile against
The power of the sea.

TO A PIECE OF CORNBREAD

I went to dine with country friends
And view the Blue Ridge Mountains,
To watch the sun set in the west
And stars light up their fountains.

I thought I'd have a pleasant chat
And give my heart some poundings,

And play a bit of this and that
In these ideal surroundings.

Now all of this occurred and more,
Without economizing;
And yet 'twas something that I ate
That calls for eulogizing.

It was a piece of cornbread brown
That gave me all this pleasure;
'Twas baked in best Virginia style,
A veritable treasure.

'Twas not too wet, 'twas not too dry,
'Twas of the right consistence;
I did not eat it all because
'Twas kept beyond my distance.

And I would dine with them again
(For each one is a winner),
But I would go with extra speed
If cornbread were for dinner.

LINES WRITTEN AS THE NINTH
OF A GROUP OF TEN MARRIES

Ten little bull-frogs sat on a bank,
Feeling so happy and free,
Scorning the waters that beckoned them in
To the sea of matrimony.

Singly in turn they quietly fell,
Plunging into the water,
Reveling there in marital bliss,
United with somebody's daughter.

One little froggie, alone on the bank,
Unhappy in being so free—
"Zounds!" said the froggie,
"I think I shall jump
To avoid my own company."

WOMEN COMBAT

HELICOPTER PILOTS

Ever since that Meg Ryan movie, the one with Denzel Washington and she played the heroic pilot of a combat helicopter, Barbara and I have been having this same discussion. It starts out something like this:

I could have done that. I wish I had been allowed to do that. But when I was still young enough to do that, they wouldn't let you, of course.

And with good reason, I thought. Women have no business volunteering to kill people. It simply isn't womanly.

I wouldn't be volunteering to kill people. I think women should be allowed to fly helicopters if they want to. And under any conditions under which men fly them. That's the point.

Then fly for Petroleum Helicopters, I would say. Or Air Logistics. Fly guys into the Gulf to work. Why does it have to be a combat helicopter?

Because they wouldn't let me do it. That's why. It has nothing to do with killing people.

Well, yes, it does, I would reply. You can't want to take on a combat assignment without wanting to kill people. You wouldn't prove effective if it came to that. Are you trying to tell me that you really want to kill people?

But who said anything about combat anyway? I just said I ought to be allowed to fly the damn helicopter if I wanted to. Just because I'm a woman doesn't mean I couldn't do it.

And on and on it would go until we tired of it. As we would of course. Discourse for the sake of discourse simply isn't worth it. Two people are always going to have areas where they can't agree. So just leave them be. When you've both said your pieces, just leave it alone.

But in my head I never could. Perhaps she simply did not understand what I was saying. If she ever did such a thing, you know, she'd have to go through basic first. And for a would-be combat soldier, male generally, but, for the sake of argument, let's suppose female, basic has failed its mission, if it does not instill in him or her the desire to use his or her weapon, given the chance. You cannot be a good soldier if you lack the desire to destroy the enemy. Destroy means kill. The enemy is alive. You cannot destroy life without killing it.

I remember a TV show I saw recently. You know, ever since affirmative action, or maybe even before, they've been so careful to put so-called minority folks in high places. On the cop shows the lieutenant always seems to be black, for instance. And on the court shows half the judges are black and/or female besides. So far the blacks seem to have the edge but the Asians and the Hispanics aren't far behind. And, God bless 'em, the women.

Anyway, here was this TV show and in one scene there was a bunch of generals and admirals all at the ready to tell the president what he should do. And, so help me, if there wasn't a decorated female general wearing the combat infantry badge! Now how do you suppose they thought she got that? There's only one way, of course. You have to have been there. In combat, I mean.

Yet, somehow, I just can't think of combat as a womanly activity. I can't argue with defending one's life, loved ones or even property. I can see a woman taking lethal action in that effort as well as a man. And I can understand murder, premeditated or as a crime of passion. But military combat is different. For one thing, one is not always on the defensive. Offense is what wins wars. And I simply do not believe it's in a true woman's genetic make-up to be a willing participant in a military offensive action. It goes against the genetic grain, I think.

I don't know. Maybe Barbara believes that combat helicopters attack only tanks. And because you can't see the people inside the tank in a combat situation, it doesn't seem like you're disintegrating them or frying them alive in there. You're only attacking the tank. Much as many fighter pilots, I imagine, may enjoy shooting down the enemy airplane but give little thought to the human pilot inside it..

The End

Printed in the United States
6446

9 781401 013677